URBAN HIGH SCHOOLS

To Rebecca, travelor a fellow traveler and dear friend [handwritten inscription] *AB Hemmings* [signature]

This multidisciplinary overview introduces readers to the historical, sociological, anthropological, and political foundations of urban public secondary schooling and to possibilities for reform. Focused on critical and problematic elements, it provides a comprehensive description and analyses of urban public high schooling through different yet intertwined disciplinary lenses. Students and researchers seeking to inform their work with urban high schools from social, cultural, and political perspectives will find the theoretical frameworks and practical applications useful in their own studies of, or initiatives related to, urban public high schools. Each chapter includes concept boxes with synopses of key ideas, summations, and discussion questions.

Annette B. Hemmings is Professor, School of Education, Edgewood College.

Sociocultural, Political, and Historical Studies in Education

Joel Spring, Editor

For additional information on titles in the Sociocultural, Political, and Historical Studies in Education series visit **www.routledge.com/education**

URBAN HIGH SCHOOLS

Foundations and Possibilities

Annette Hemmings
EDGEWOOD COLLEGE

Routledge
Taylor & Francis Group

NEW YORK AND LONDON

First published 2012
by Routledge
711 Third Avenue, New York, NY 10017

Simultaneously published in the UK
by Routledge
2 Park Square, Milton Park, Abingdon, Oxon OX14 4RN

Routledge is an imprint of the Taylor & Francis Group, an informa business

Library of Congress Cataloging in Publication Data
Hemmings, Annette B.
    Urban high schools : foundations and possibilities / Annette Hemmings.
    p. cm. — (Sociocultural, political, and historical studies in education)
    Includes bibliographical references and index.
    1. Urban high schools—United States. I. Title.
    LC5131.H36 2011
    373.09173'2—dc23
    2011031629

ISBN: 978-0-415-87870-8 (hbk)
ISBN: 978-0-415-87871-5 (pbk)
ISBN: 978-0-203-83237-0 (ebk)

Typeset in Bembo and Stone Sans
by EvS Communication Networx, Inc.

Printed and bound in the United States of America on acid-free paper
by Walsworth Publishing Company, Marceline, MO.

SUSTAINABLE FORESTRY INITIATIVE
Certified Sourcing
www.sfiprogram.org
SFI-00555
The SFI label applies to the text stock.

CONTENTS

PREFACE

Urban public high schools located in U.S. cities, which are at the nexus of national and global commerce, culture, and communication, are among the few places where young people from all walks of life can come together, learn together, and ideally mesh together. Funded and regulated by the federal government, states, and local communities, they are institutions where teachers are hired to provide adolescents who have different interests and needs, and come from different racial, ethnic, social class, and gendered backgrounds with the formal education they need to prosper as individuals; find gainful employment in competitive job markets; participate in the social and cultural life of their communities; and make worthwhile contributions as members of a democratic citizenry. Urban public high schools are vital institutions with diverse student populations, multiple goals, and many means for accomplishing important educational ends. They deserve, and must have, utmost public support.

And yet, these schools are plagued with high dropout rates, low test scores, ill-prepared teachers, violence, and other daunting challenges that have eroded public commitment to them. Urban public high schools should be nurturing our greatest hopes but are, instead, arousing our gravest concerns. They have been targets of numerous reforms, but outcomes are often disappointing or simply unsustainable.

Educational historians, sociologists of education, educational anthropologists, and political scientists interested in education provide distinct yet interrelated disciplinary perspectives on urban public high schools that illuminate their workings and challenges. They study these schools as complex organizations embedded in multilayered contexts where school administrators and teachers are expected to educate adolescents who are among the most diverse in the nation. While these scholars are interested in explicating schooling processes, most of them are also deeply concerned about the persistence of seemingly intractable problems and injustices related to urban public high schools' organization, high numbers of alienated working-class, low-income, racial and ethnic minority students, and teachers who lack the resources and preparation they need to address the everyday classroom challenges they face. They offer incisive insights on these and other problems, and inform solutions to them.

Divided into two parts, "Foundations" and "Possibilities," this book introduces readers to the historical, sociological, anthropological, and political foundations of, and reform possibilities for, urban public high schools in the United States.

Part I, "Foundations," begins with chapter 1 on the *historical contexts* of U.S. urban public high schools since the 1960s. It describes how these schools have been altered overtime by shifting population demographics; economic conditions and transformations; the Civil Rights movement and desegregation; bilingual and special education legislation; sociocultural revolutions; reform movements; and other historical events.

Chapter 2, focusing on *sociological basics,* describes the relationship between urban public schools and society; the critical importance of social class and intersections with race, ethnicity, and gender; and economic, cultural, social, and symbolic capital in educational pursuits. Urban public high schools are then elucidated as semibureaucratic organizations with variable goals, uncertain technologies, tightly and loosely coupled structures, and unstable authority relations. School organizational culture and subcultures are described as social constructions that constitute the most essential localized understandings informing the roles, identities, and actions of administrators, teachers, and students.

Chapter 3 offers *anthropological perspectives* on urban high schools. Schools are conceived as sites where the mainstream cultural commitments of Anglo/ European middle-class groups are reaffirmed and transmitted through processes of enculturation and acculturation. Adaptations associated with students' cultural identity work are explored as especially crucial for academic achievement because of the considerable impact identity has on whether or how diverse youths accommodate, resist, or otherwise adapt to schooling processes. Cultural identity work in urban high schools is closely connected to what it means to be an "educated person"—a symbolic figure fashioned by cultural criteria that identify people as more, or less, knowledgeable. Cultural processes, including student cultural identity work, are key elements in a steady procession of theoretical frameworks on racial and ethnic student achievement that run the historical gamut from cultural deficit theories that prevailed in the 1960s to home–school cultural discontinuity, new cultural pluralism, cultural–ecological, segmented assimilation, and racial formation theories. Also discussed is the influence of religion and cultural challenges faced by Jewish, Muslim, and other religious minorities. The chapter concludes with how researchers and school actors can engage in cultural productions with constructive pedagogical implications.

Chapter 4 on *political insights* sheds light on the politics of public education and urban public high schools. Ideology and its influences are defined followed by a discussion of national politics with a focus on how Democratic and Republican Party ideologies have shaped federal educational policies and legislation related to urban public high schools, and also on the national agendas of teacher unions. There is also discussion of midlevel politics that involve school districts and regional external partners with attention to the logics of sociopolitical relations. This discussion is followed by an examination of school-level governance models and the crucial importance of relational trust, and the politics of everyday life played out in classroom ecologies of games and corridor contests over the power of respect.

Part II, "Possibilities," explores possibilities for urban public high school reform with historical, sociological, anthropological, and political foundations in mind. Chapter 5 sets *local school staging areas* for reform through descriptions and analyses of urban public high schools as construction sites for successful or futile schooling. District and local school actors—principals, teachers, students, school board members, union officials, superintendents, parents, and external partners—are depicted as agents of positive change or hopeless defeat; conservators of sensible or incapacitating practices; and pragmatically adaptive or cynically resistant to external directives. Principals are responsible for setting directions, running daily organizational operations, making sure teachers are providing good instruction, and enforcing student disciplinary, safety, and other policies. They are the point men and women in the middle of politically tricky, sometimes contentious relations within their schools and with district central offices and unions. Teachers for their part negotiate a number of roles including classroom instruction, outside classroom duties, supervision of extracurricular activities, and possibly administration and quasi-parenting. They must establish their authority in relation to students; deal with inadequate resources; and handle a constant barrage of outside directives. Any or all of this can lead to burnout. Students in their roles are expected to comply with rules, teachers' orders, and the classroom schoolwork regimens that structure academic activities and discipline. Their compliance is affected by schoolwork regimens, and also by sociocultural locations; socioeconomic conditions; youth culture and peer-group subcultures; and cultural identity work. School boards, unions, superintendents, parents, and external partners also play important supporting roles. Also described in chapter 5 are classroom, corridor, and principal dramas which depict how demoralized many urban public high schools are with their disabling organizational cultures and dysfunctional structures. These schools are staging areas for the institutionalization of failure. Despite this disheartening reality, they can be reenvisioned for the realization of reform possibilities.

Chapter 6 focuses on *urban public high school reform*. It begins with a discussion of the fundamental facts of schooling: classroom dynamics; school organizational cultures, structures and moral orders; principal leadership; local community characteristics; federal, state, and district educational directives; and multi-institutional partnerships. The most ideal reforms are those that reenvision planning and implementation change processes, and attend to school reculturation, restructuring, and remoralization with fundamental facts of schooling in mind. Reculturation occurs when school actors engage in cultural productions intentionally geared toward the construction of outward expressions, behavioral norms, and values that engender and sustain effective schooling. Restructuring may involve changes in structures affecting the formal roles and responsibilities of school actors, professional community teams, scheduling, and governance in ways that support pedagogical ingenuity, teamwork, shared decision making, and student achievement. Remoralization entails collective moral and ethical commitment to worthwhile curriculum, proper pedagogy and good character. Reenvisioning, reculturation, restructuring, and remoralization should be taken into consideration in urban public high school possibilities for reform that are genuinely and practically aimed at providing all students with excellent and equitable educations.

PART I

Foundations

Urban high schools are among the most essential yet troubled institutions in the United States. The largest 100 urban school districts constitute less than 1/10th of 1% of the over 17,000 districts in the United States, but they serve 25% of all public school students. Forty percent of students of color and a third of all students from low-income families attend urban public schools (Education Commission of the States, 2003). Far too many high schools in urban districts are characterized by cumbersome bureaucratic structures and chronic underfunding (Fine, 1994a; Weiner, 2000); high concentrations of disaffected low-income, immigrant, and "involuntary minority" students (Ogbu, 1991, 1987, 1978; Seller & Weis, 1998); high drop-out rates and low standardized test scores (Fine, 1991); high teacher turnover (Ingersoll, 2001); and intergroup student conflict that can lead to violent confrontations (Adams, 1999; Giroux, 1998; Hemmings, 2000a, 2002, 2003). There are compelling social and economic arguments for investing in urban public high schools as essential parts of the equation for ensuring the future of urban centers. We also need to bolster them as sites where teenagers can come of age as young adults who not only prosper as individuals, but are also morally vested in contributing to the common good (Hemmings, 2004).

Many researchers and policymakers focus on teacher qualifications, student characteristics, curricular content, and other discrete aspects of urban public schooling in a manner that does not take historical, social, cultural, and political forces into account. Historians for their part have written invaluable accounts illuminating the considerable and enduring impact that past events have had on contemporary public schools. Their accounts offer incisive histories of the social, cultural, political, economic, judicial, legal, and legislative contexts within which urban high schools have taken shape. These contexts are constantly changing in ways that are not necessarily beneficial for urban high schools and have proved, at times, to be quite deleterious.

Sociologists of education have long acknowledged the close relationship between schools and society, and they have examined issues related to formal schooling at the societal, institutional, interpersonal, and intrapsychic levels (Persell, 1977). Those interested in the societal level explicate the role that schools play in socializing and sorting young people into the status quo of a hierarchically stratified socioeconomic system. Other sociologists focus on institutional-level school organization; the importance of cultural, social, and symbolic capital; organizational culture and subcultures; teacher–student and student–student relations; and how schooling processes are social constructions shaped in part by the powerful influences of societal and institutional forces on teachers' and students' attitudes toward schooling. Nearly all sociologists of education in their theorizing and empirical research are deeply if not primarily concerned with how socioeconomic inequalities are generated and possibly ameliorated in public high schools, especially those serving historically marginalized youths.

Educational anthropologists are interested in culture broadly defined as the patterns of behavior adopted by social groups. From an anthropological perspective, high schools in the United States are essentially established to transmit dominant "mainstream" cultural commitments. These commitments are steeped in Anglo/European traditions and middle-class interests, and include notions of what it means to be an "educated person" widely recognized as someone with valued cultural competencies and academic knowledge (Levinson & Holland, 1996). High schools become sites for cross-cultural conflict when cultural differences, especially those expressed by racial and ethnic minority groups, clash with one another and with dominant cultural prescriptions. This is likely to happen in urban high schools serving multiracial and multiethnic student populations where conflict over the meaning of education and what it means to belong to particular groups is fueled by cultural identities, community and home cultural commitments, and tensions fueled by a long history of discrimination. Cultural identity work has an especially profound impact on whether or how adolescent students accommodate to, or resist, schooling. Many contemporary educational anthropologists view schools as places where students, teachers, administrators, and other school actors engage in cultural productions that can reinforce, impede, or transform identities and schooling processes.

Political scientists interested in urban secondary education are concerned with power, power relations, and how groups vie for power in various educational and school arenas. They explore macrolevel politics and the powerful influence that Democratic and Republican Party ideologies have on educational policies and legislation. Also crucial are politics at state, regional, and district levels which not only involve offices directly responsible for the management of schools, but also teacher unions, corporations, industries, institutions of higher education (IHE), and other community agencies. While these organizations share a common interest in effective urban public schooling, they can become embroiled in thorny political disputes over decision making, resources, and administration in light of their own more particular interests. Politics also play out at the school level where administrators, teachers, and students vie to maximize their political advantages and dominance and minimize the power of competing groups through formal governance processes as well as the more informal politics of everyday life in classrooms and corridors. A more thorough exploration of these and other dynamics begins with the historical context of urban public high schools.

1

HISTORICAL CONTEXTS

There is a longstanding debate in education over whether public schools are inflexibly structured by society or whether society can be progressively transformed through its schools. The historical fact of the matter is that public schools are directly affected by the social, cultural, political, economic, judicial, legal, and legislative contexts within which they are embedded. They must adapt to these contexts if they have any chance of providing young people with the formal educations they need to thrive in, make meaningful contributions to, and perhaps revolutionize society. Schools change, for better or worse, as a consequence of changes in societal contexts. This is certainly true for urban public high schools, which, as the following historical narrative elucidates, have experienced the most challenging, sometimes devastating effects of change.

1900 to the 1950s

A momentous economic and demographic transition occurred between 1900 and World War II that left a permanent mark on urban public high schools, especially with regard to the demographics of the students they served. The United States was transformed during this period from a largely agrarian society into one characterized by industrialization and the rapid growth of cities. The United States became the foremost producer of manufactured goods, which spurred a need for large numbers of factory, construction, and other blue-collar workers. Waves of immigrant workers and their families fueled the expansion of American cities. Immigrants were densely concentrated in urban areas, and viewed by many older White inhabitants with Anglo/European backgrounds as foreign, alien, and threats to traditional American values. Immigrants were a particular cause for concern among city officials who wanted to make sure that new arrivals from other countries were assimilated or "Americanized" into U.S. society (Tyack, 1974).

Immigration eventually leveled off, but beginning in the 1920s, there was a steady and significant migration of Black Americans from the South to the North. Only a third of Blacks lived in cities in 1920. Forty years later, almost three-fourths were residing in large urban centers that included Northern manufacturing metropolises in New England and the Midwestern states. Black migration to the North carried deep racial divisions from the South, which made residential segregation more extreme and intensified fears among Anglo/European Americans about forging a shared culture in the United States (Bankston & Caldas, 2009).

Urban public schools were identified as prime sites for Americanization and also for preparing youth for the industrial workforce. From World War II to the present, these schools have enrolled large numbers of racially and ethnically diverse students from low-income and working-class backgrounds while, at the same time, serving the children and interests of Anglo/European White middle-class families. Sociocultural and economic divides led to school segregation that was mostly by law (de jure) in the South and a consequence of segregated residential patterns (de facto) in the North. For the most part, middle-class White urbanites sent their children to one set of public schools and other students, most notably Black Americans, attended different schools. In keeping with judicial rulings and laws of the time, public schools could be racially separate but had to be equal. Separate but equal schooling never occurred because of significant disparities in resources, curricular offerings, facilities, staff, and length of the school year. Schools serving middle-class White students were, simply put, much better than those enrolling Black children.

There was an organized effort in the 1940s to use the judicial system to end school segregation and this eventually resulted in the landmark Supreme Court decision *Brown v. Board of Education* in 1954 (Cross, 2004). The *Brown* decision declared state laws establishing separate public schools for Black and White children unconstitutional and overturned the *Plessy v. Ferguson* decision of 1896 which permitted school segregation (Caldas & Bankston, 2008; deMarrais & LeCompte, 1999). The Court anticipated that the *Brown* decision would move public school systems away from the "separate but equal" doctrine that had held sway since the *Plessy* decision. Justices hoped their ruling would provide equal educational opportunities for Black Americans through desegregated schooling. The ruling also set an important precedent for the use of social science research in legal considerations of educational inequality (Wong & Nicotera, 2004). But public school segregation did not end with the *Brown* decision and persisted into the 1960s when other momentous changes finally turned the tide.

1960s

The 1960s began as a time of economic prosperity in the United States. The economy during this decade began to shift from an industrial blue-collar base to a postindustrial white-collar one with increasing demands for workers with technical and information management skills, high functional literacy, and more specialized office proficiencies (Bankston & Caldas, 2009). Formal education, especially postsecondary educational degrees and credentials, were increasingly more important for future workers and their employers. It was not surprising given this trend that there was a notable escalation in efforts to end the long legacy of inequitable K-12 schooling. Public schools, especially those located in racially and ethnically diverse urban centers, were again targeted as prime institutions for preparing students for jobs in the new economy and also, in a significant historical twist, putting an end to socioeconomic inequalities and injustices.

Changes in judicial and legislative contexts related to educational equity were augmented by a cultural revolution induced in part by the advent of television and other technological advancements. Marwick (1998) portrays the 1960s as a time of renaissance when new and imaginative artistic forms were born, and intellectual and social experimentation became vogue. While many people during this period still expected public schools to Americanize all children, another emergent expectation was that they offer equal educational opportunities to all students regardless of their racial, ethnic, and social class backgrounds. Equal access to a good education became a driving force in social causes that influenced changes in judicial and legislative contexts. This expectation was an impetus for the civil rights movement and created the political context for the passage of the Civil Rights Act in 1964 (Cross 2004; Orfield, 2000).

As Orfield (2000) astutely observes, the 1964 Civil Rights Act had more impact on American education than any other federal education law in the 20th century. This historical fact is rarely considered in discussions of contemporary education policy especially with regard to how the act framed civil rights responsibilities in public school operations.

One of the most significant consequences of the 1964 law was the desegregation of Southern schools. The Southern system of school segregation was declared unconstitutional by the Supreme Court in 1954, but Southern resistance was so intense that enforcement of the *Brown* decision through private lawsuits was unsuccessful. The 1964 Civil Rights Act was the enforcement arm that finally put an end to segregation in the South and it did so within 5 years. It squelched "generations of legally imposed apartheid" in the South (Orfield, 2000, p. 89).

The 1964 law also addressed other forms of educational discrimination in the following ways:

1. It provided the Justice Department with the authority to file civil rights litigation, which gave the Civil Rights Division much greater influence in shaping the agenda of civil rights law and greatly increased the resources available to initiate civil rights cases.
2. It established mandatory fund cutoffs, ending federal aid to discriminatory school districts through administrative processes (Title VI).
3. It authorized research and monitoring, including a national study and report to Congress on school desegregation, a 4-year extension of the Civil Rights Commission, and a broadening of the commission's functions (Titles IV and V).
4. It funded technical assistance and teacher training to ease the transition to desegregated schools (Title IV).
5. It supported community conciliation and help in dealing with racial tensions through establishment of Community Relations Services (Title X).
6. It prohibited job discrimination at the federal level (Title VII), which did not originally apply to teachers but did so after the law was strengthened in 1972. (Orfield, 2000, p. 92)

The 1964 Civil Rights Act was passed at the same time that President Lyndon Johnson was waging what became known as his War on Poverty. This movement also yielded significant legislation. A concern for supporters was the widespread and persistent school achievement gap between Black children living in poverty and other children. President Johnson and Democrats in Congress put together and passed a package of social welfare legislation with the claim that it "would end poverty in our time." The package was premised on the assumption that there was a culture of poverty in impoverished Black communities that kept Black people in a perpetual state of poverty. Supporters believed that government programs could eliminate poverty by changing the cultures of poor Black people. The War on Poverty thus had a great deal in common with the Americanization movement of the early 20th century which

---

CONCEPT BOX 1.1

1960s Key Legislation

1964 Civil Rights Act: Legislative enforcement arm that was instrumental in ending de jure school desegregation in the South and addressing other forms of racial discrimination.

1965 Elementary and Secondary Education Act (ESEA): Legislation establishing compensatory education programs based on the speculation that poverty and the racial achievement gap could be lessened through programs that compensate for the historical disadvantages and cultural deprivations of poor Black children.

was, and remains, a major theme in the history of public schools (Bankston & Caldas, 2009).

One of the most important pieces of legislation in the package was the Elementary and Secondary Education Act (ESEA) of 1965 (Cross, 2004). The ESEA was based on the speculation that poverty and the racial achievement gap could be lessened through programs that compensated for the historical disadvantages and cultural deprivations of poor Black children. A key provision was Title I which distributed funds to schools and school districts with high percentages of low-income students. Schools, especially those in urban areas, were flooded with funding for ESEA programs including remedial reading and other compensatory interventions.

The Upward Bound program was also established through federal legislation. This program was aimed at low-income high school students and was part of the Higher Education Act of 1965. The goal of Upward Bound is to provide disadvantaged students with better opportunities for going to college. Qualified students are admitted to 6-week summer programs where they take college prep courses and acquire work experience. They also receive weekly follow-up and tutoring during the regular school year.

Other more conservative historians concede there was a momentous cultural revolution in the 1960s that changed legislative, judicial, and political contexts in ways that caused lawmakers, judges, and policymakers to be more determined in their efforts to desegregate public schools; ensure that all children had equal access to a good education; and provide low-income Black students in public schools with federally funded compensatory education programs if they needed them. But these historians also maintain that the changes undermined rather than upheld traditional American values (Americanization) and essential academic curriculum and standards in ways that threatened the cultural and scholastic foundation of public schooling in the United States (Kimball, 2000). An ideological split emerged between those who welcomed the cultural transformations and those who wanted to preserve what they regarded as national cultural and curricular traditions.

Cultural transformations spilled over into the 1970s and fed into stepped up judicial efforts to put an end to school desegregation and other injustices related to equal access to educational opportunities. The results of these efforts permanently changed urban public high schools.

1970s

The 1964 Civil Rights Act was instrumental in ending de jure public school segregation in the South, but had little impact on de facto residential and school segregation in the North. It was during the late 1960s and throughout the 1970s that school desegregation in both the North and South was enforced or, some would say, forced. It was the Supreme Court, not federal or state legislatures, which drove the effort. In 1968, the Court handed down the watershed *Green* decision (*Green v. County School Board;* McGuinn, 2006). The case involved districts in Virginia with a freedom-of-choice desegregation plan that did not result in the racial integration of schools. Because White families did not choose to send their children to Black schools, the Court ruled the state was still operating an unconstitutional segregated school system. The school system was ordered to implement a plan that would integrate public schools and do so immediately. Three years later, the Supreme Court in the *Swann v. Charlotte-Mecklenburg Board of Education* case upheld the constitutionality of busing to create racially mixed schools (Caldas & Bankston, 2008). After another landmark case referred to as the *Denver* decision (*Keys v. School District Number 1*, 1973), court orders were handed down in many Northern cities that required them to reveal histories of discrimination and to integrate schools effectively if they were racially segregated. Suburbs were virtually exempted by a Supreme Court decision in 1974 that essentially spared them from desegregation (Orfield, 2000).

Desegregation was occurring alongside the relaxation of traditional school norms in the aftermath of the cultural revolution. The strict moral and behavior standards that had characterized many urban public high schools eroded. Boys were no longer required to wear dress shirts and slacks, and girls were allowed to wear pants. Hallway behavior was not monitored as closely as it had once been, and racially and ethnically diverse students suddenly thrown together were somehow expected to get along despite a long history of intergroup conflict. The sale and consumption of marijuana, heroin, crack cocaine, and other illicit drugs soared. Many students became members of drug sub-

---

CONCEPT BOX 1.2

School Desegregation Court Rulings

1954 Brown v. Board of Education: State laws establishing separate public schools for Black and White students declared unconstitutional. Ruling overturned 1896 *Plessy v. Ferguson* decision permitting "separate but equal" school segregation.

1968 Green v. County School Board: Declared freedom-of-choice desegregation plans unconstitutional. Virginia school systems ordered to implement plans that effectively ended school desegregation.

1971 Swann v. Charlotte-Mecklenburg Board of Education: Upheld the constitutionality of busing as a remedy for desegregating public schools.

1973 Keys v. School District Number 1 (Denver decision): Districts had to prove histories of discrimination and integration of public schools that were racially segregated.

cultures, which they openly expressed through clothing and hair styles, slang and lingo, music, and various insignia. These subcultures cut across social class and racial and ethnic peer groups. Significant changes also occurred in mores related to teenage pregnancy. Before 1970, teenage girls who became pregnant out of wedlock were removed from school. By the end of the 1970s, they were allowed to stay in school and graduate with their classmates.

Internal sociocultural organizational changes reflected larger societal trends that made it much more difficult for urban public high schools to withstand the externally mandated changes brought about by Supreme Court rulings and orders. These changes along with many others swept through urban high schools so rapidly that they rocked the cultural moorings that had stabilized life in classrooms and corridors leaving chaos and confusion in their wake (Gonsalves & Leonard, 2007).

The destabilization of school cultures was exacerbated by desegregation orders hastily imposed by courts that did not understand the ethos and operational dynamics of public high schools. Conflict over the hurried mandatory busing plans included in many desegregation plans led to "White flight" or, more accurately, the flight of middle-class families from urban public schools. These families moved to suburbs or turned to private schools because they feared the loss of safety and good educational opportunities for their children (Orfield, Eaton, & the Harvard Project on Desegregation, 1996).

Bilingual education was also introduced by judicial and legislative decrees in the 1970s. The Bilingual Education Act was passed in 1968 with assurances that the cultures and natal languages of Native Americans, Mexican Americans, Puerto Ricans, and other ethnic groups speaking English as their second language would be preserved by the public schools. Implementation of bilingual education programs in public schools was virtually mandatory after the 1974 U.S. Supreme Court decision in *Lau et al. v. Nichols et al.* (Spring, 2010). This case was a class-action suit brought for non-English-speaking Chinese students in the San Francisco school district where no special instruction for learning Standard English was provided for them. *Lau* remedies required public schools

CONCEPT BOX 1.3

Bilingual Education

1968 Bilingual Education Act: Legislation with public school bilingual education programs that assured the preservation of the cultures and natal languages of ethnic groups speaking English as their second language.

1974 Lau et al. v. Nichols et al.: Public schools were required to assist limited English speaking students through instruction in students' native tongues in some academic courses.

CONCEPT BOX 1.4

Special Education

Federal and state laws passed in the 1970s require students with special needs attending public schools to be educated in least restrictive environments. The laws give parents the right to question their child's placements and require schools to develop and maintain an individual education plan (IEP) for each student with special needs.

---

to assist students who spoke limited English through instruction in students' native tongues in some academic courses. Remedies mandated bilingual education for schools having at least 20 limited English speakers of the same minority group (Spring, 2010).

In addition to these changes was the passage of federal and state laws that required students with special needs attending public schools to be educated in least restrictive environments. The law gave parents more rights to question their child's placements and required schools to develop and maintain an individual education plan (IEP) for each student with special needs. Students with special needs were also given greater access to regular education classrooms.

The implementation of this legislation created friction between special education and regular education teachers who were ill-prepared for the inclusion of special needs students in regular classrooms. Professional development was virtually nonexistent in the 1970s, which meant that teachers had to figure out on their own how to provide rigorous academic instruction while, at the same time, accommodating students with limited English proficiencies and special needs.

Urban public high school staff and students in the 1970s were overwhelmed with changes imposed on them by courts and legislatures, and also by larger societal changes. The decade was a period when urban schools serving racially and ethnically diverse students were radically transformed in intended and unintended ways. Teachers had to cope with new requirements and with students who came to their classes with a much wider range of aptitude for, and faith in, formal education. Many teachers "dummied down" the curriculum and their instructional practices in defensive attempts to maintain some modicum of order in disorderly classroom environments (McNeil, 1983). They were besieged with the multitude and magnitude of changes, and did not receive the professional development and support they needed to adjust to the overwhelming challenges they confronted. The situation worsened in the 1980s when student achievement plummeted, raising concerns among legislators and business leaders.

1980s to the Present

Urban public school districts in the 1980s moved away from desegregation plans with mandatory busing and other remedies that gave families little or no choice in schools. They adopted more voluntary plans featuring magnet schools with programs that would appeal to students with specialized interests. Students could choose and apply for admittance to a program in accordance with district-wide application and admission procedures. Different schools in different parts of cities offered programs in the arts, technical and vocational fields, college preparation, and other areas. The aim was not only to end the resistance and anger caused by hastily implemented desegregation plans, but also to attract middle-class families back to public high schools.

Middle-class families were especially drawn to rigorous college prep programs, such as those that included Advanced Placement (AP) courses or offered the International Baccalaureate curriculum. Some of these programs were system-wide or an option within a school. Public high schools were under pressure to show a numerical balance of White students and students of color in their programs so many of them set up a quota system with seats reserved for students from underrepresented groups. The schools were also required to accommodate students with special needs, offer bilingual education programs, and otherwise comply with court orders and laws.

While many urban public high schools in the early 1980s appeared to be desegregated based on enrollment demographics, a significant number became internally resegregated as middle-class White students became disproportionately overrepresented in college preparatory and upper-track classes, and Black students, Latinos,[1] and other students of color dominated remedial, special education, bilingual education, and other low-level classes.

Urban public high schools were further resegregated over time as White middle-class families lost interest in what the schools offered. There has been a steady rise in the proportion of racial and ethnic minority students. Although Black and Latino children are minorities in the overall population of the United States, they made up over 60% of urban public school students by 2000 (Bankston & Caldas, 2009). In some urban high schools they constitute over 90% of the student population.

School desegregation as a hotly contested national and state issue virtually disappeared in the 1990s. Other concerns arose that included the devastating effects of the postindustrial economic shift on working-class men, especially those residing in inner cities. Until the 1980s, men with or without high school diplomas were able to find good blue-collar jobs in manufacturing plants, semi-skilled trades, and other industries. The most sought after jobs usually went to White men who were major beneficiaries of employment in the industrial labor market (Fine & Weis, 1998). Black men were more typically hired to do the dirtiest or most dangerous work but many of them also managed to earn a living wage. Both categories of jobs were outsourced to other countries in the 1990s, and many of the employment opportunities that became available were geared toward the production and marketing of information, communications, consumer goods, and services. These jobs, especially those in the service sector, did not provide men with the high levels of pay their forebears had earned during the decades of the industrial labor market.

Fine and Weis (1998) in their study of the lives of poor and working-class youth in the postindustrial age found White boys mired in a "discourse of loss" brought about by the decline in the "truly masculine jobs" that had provided their fathers and grandfathers with enough money and manly status to secure dominant positions in their homes and other social spheres (p. 39). The impact on youth of color was much worse and more demoralizing. African American and Latino young men were finding it increasingly difficult to get good jobs and felt they were being hindered by discrimination, racism, and disinvestment in the places where they lived. Wilson (1996) in his comprehensive study of the new urban poor describes the steady loss of jobs in inner cities and the socially destructive effects that male joblessness has had on urban neighborhoods. The decline in legitimate employment opportunities among inner-city residents increased incentives for male adolescents and young men to engage in drug trafficking and other illicit ventures to acquire money and status. Many of them joined street gangs that were heavily involved in the underground economy and there was a significant upsurge in murder rates and other criminal acts of violence.

> Between 1985 and 1992, there was a sharp increase in the murder rate among men under the age of 24; for men 18 years old and younger, murder rates doubled. Black males in particular have been involved in this upsurge in violence. For example, whereas the homicide rate for white males between 14 and 17 increased from 8 per 100,000 in 1984 to 14 in 1991, the rate for Black males tripled during that time (from 32 per 100,000 to 112). This sharp rise in violent crime among younger males… accompanied the widespread outbreak of addiction to crack cocaine. The association is especially strong in inner-city ghetto neighborhoods plagued by joblessness and weak social organization. (Wilson, 1996, p. 21)

There was a severe economic recession in 1988 that increased inner-city unemployment rates even more, and also led to deep cuts in urban public high school budgets. Programs were cut back or canceled; teaching and administrative forces were reduced; and facility maintenance was neglected. Students had to contend with overcrowded classrooms, lackluster curriculum and instruction, textbook and instructional supply shortages, dilapidated buildings, and demoralized teachers with low or no expectations for them.

Violence inside and outside of urban public high schools escalated. School cultures sank to toxic levels as members of street gangs or other adversarial groups clashed in classrooms, corridors, and playgrounds. Fights were common with occasional deadly shootings. Violence was shattering whatever morale was left. Teachers gave up on students and students gave up on schooling.

Hope for the seemingly hopeless situation of urban public high schools was afforded in the 1990s through partnerships between private businesses and public schools. Such partnerships were regarded by policymakers and members of Congress as vital if not essential for rebuilding depressed urban economies and broken educational systems. In 1994, Congress passed the School-to-Work Opportunities Act (SWOA) which included a framework for the development of a national school-to-work program. The act encouraged voluntary collaborations between businesses and schools where business personnel worked with educators on school reform that integrated academic requirements with regional job opportunities. A relatively small amount of federal dollars was allocated for the SWOA and there was no guarantee that grants awarded to states would actually result in a national school-to-work program. The SWOA was nevertheless regarded as crucial for addressing the overall problem of wage inequities and economic marginality among low-income groups, especially impoverished inner-city youth. It was viewed as an important weapon in the fight against acute joblessness (Wilson, 1996).

The SWOA was one of many efforts involving partnerships between businesses and schools. District councils and other associations were created in the 1990s and 2000s for the express purpose of pairing up businesses with urban high schools in the development, implementation, and resourcing of programs that would create pathways to the workplace or higher education. Business leaders in their collaborations with urban public high schools became increasingly frustrated with what they saw. Many schools were so dysfunctional and students were so poorly educated that they were virtually unemployable. The leaders wanted, and began to lobby for, standards of accountability that would utilize standardized testing and other means in business–oriented assessment systems that would measure public schools' success and failure rates, and also hold public schools accountable for educational outcomes.

Advances in testing theory, statistics, and computing capacity made this possible. New and complex mathematical models for assessment led to the

---

CONCEPT BOX 1.5

1990s Partnerships

1994 School-to-Work Opportunities Act (SWOA): The SWOA provided grants that funded voluntary collaborations between businesses and schools in the design and implementation of programs that integrated academic requirements with job opportunities in regional development of value-added statistics that could be used to measure how much of a student's learning (output) is due to classroom instruction and school environments (inputs) in ways that controlled for a multitude of extraneous variables. Value-added assessment techniques were derived from econometric measures originally created to measure business inputs and outputs (Kay, 1993). These techniques coupled with the technical capabilities to apply them to an entire state's school-aged population could be used to reward or rebuke teachers and schools. They became the instrumental means for raising and equalizing student achievement in a monumental educational accountability movement that swept the nation in the 1990s and early 2000s (Bankston & Caldas, 2009).

The educational accountability movement underpinned the passage of the federal No Child Left Behind legislation (NCLB; 2001) and similar legislation at the state level. Curriculum was standardized state wide. Students in benchmark grades were required to take state exams and had to repeat grades if they failed. Graduation exams were also instituted. Students had to pass these exams to receive high school diplomas even if they had passed all of their classes.

New standards were also established for teachers, including tests for licensure and professional development requirements. Schools were graded on the basis of progress and performance criteria that included student standardized test scores, and state departments of education were directed to take underperforming schools and districts into receivership. Schools with the most abysmal levels of performance were restructured or shut down. The movement also opened the door for the establishment of charter schools. These publicly funded schools operate free of district requirements but are directly accountable to the state.

Supporters of the educational accountability movement are well intentioned. A notable and important aim of the movement is to improve the educational opportunities of low-income racially and ethnically diverse students. But it has had a somewhat adverse effect on many urban public high schools. Dropout rates, already quite high grew higher as students repeatedly failed standardized

---

CONCEPT BOX 1.6

Educational Accountability Movement

National movement that prompted public school districts to adopt sophisticated assessment techniques to reward or rebuke teachers and schools. Accountability strategies led to curriculum standardization; standardized examinations required in benchmark grades; student requirements to pass graduation examinations; teacher requirements to take tests for licensure and participate in professional development; schools graded on the basis of performance criteria; and underperforming schools taken into state receivership.

tests. Good teachers who felt constrained by the new requirements or pressures to "teach to the test" left for new positions or abandoned teaching altogether. Schools were closed. Morale in low performance schools hit bottom. And any hopes of attracting middle-class students were dashed.

In 2011 countless reform efforts were underway, most of which were focused on fine tuning No Child Left Behind legislation and standardized testing, reworking curricular standards, restructuring schools, and setting up charter schools. Numerous urban public high schools are being reorganized into "schools within schools," schools offering programs involving partnerships, or places undergoing other kinds of structural renovations. Such reforms are not aimed at revamping school cultures (reculturation) the importance of which, as Gonsalves and Leonard (2007) explain, cannot nor should not be underestimated.

> Schools cannot successfully operate without cultural cohesion. The cohesive cultures of some urban high schools were so severely and utterly destroyed that it was and is impossible for them to fix themselves. We have a human problem here that we keep attempting to fix with technical solutions. Curricular standards and academic rigor alone will never help urban schools fix their broken cultures. (Gonsalves & Leonard, 2007, p. 160)

In the midst of concern about the need for cultural cohesion in public schools there was a significant demographic and accompanying sociocultural shift in many big cities. It began in 1965 after passage of Hart-Celler immigration reform legislation that ended the national origin quotas for U.S. immigration policy that had been in place since 1924. Prior to this legislation, immigrants to the United States were overwhelmingly European and White. Newcomers could now come from other parts of the world. Immigrants in the 1970s and 1980s included Dominicans, South Americans, Colombians, Ecuadorians, Peruvians, Puerto Ricans, West Indians, Chinese, Koreans, Africans, and other people not generally regarded as "White" or necessarily belonging to African American or other racially demarcated groups. There is a growing population of the children of the new wave of non-European immigrants, who are not fitting into historically entrenched cleavages between the "White" descendents of immigrants and the "Black" descendents of American slaves (Kasinitz et al., 2008). This rapidly growing group of young people, many of whom are achieving in public schools, has been changing the social and cultural tapestry of American cities. And, as Kasinitz et al. (2008) explain, members of this second generation are making significant strides in educational attainments.

> On measures of educational attainment and labor force status, two-fifths of the second generation has already gone beyond their immigrant parents. Except among Dominican men, there is little evidence of second

generation decline. In every case, the second generation young people we have studied are doing at least somewhat better than natives of the same race, even after adjusting for various advantages in family background. (p. 16)

These young people are not achieving success by remaining in their immigrant communities nor are they becoming Americanized in ways that match the profiles of Anglo/European Americans. They are using their creative energy to produce and take advantage of sociocultural innovations.

Other immigrants and their descendents at the other extreme are trying to preserve their cultures, especially their religious traditions. In the late 1970s and early 1980s, a number of families from Yemeni and other Muslim nations moved to the United States to take advantage of high-paying industrial job opportunities. Some members of this group assimilated, but others gravitated toward or maintained existing conservative Islamic religious beliefs and rituals, especially after September 11, 2001 (Sarroub, 2005). Increased conflict between the United States and militant Muslim groups is a contemporary phenomenon with profound implications for some urban high schools.

Historical changes have had notably significant effects on urban public schooling. They have had, as will be explained in the next chapter, an especially unsettling impact on the organizational functions and operations of schools.

Summation

The history of urban public high schools is a story of institutional adaptation to momentous changes in national and local social, cultural, political, economic, judicial, legal, and legislative contexts. Immigration and the migration of Black families to Northern cities during the first half of the 20th century resulted in a racially and ethnically diverse urban public school student population that persists today. Urban public high schools during this period were racially segregated—de jure in the South and de facto in the North—in school systems that were virtually sanctioned by the Supreme Court. This period was also characterized by an industrial economy that provided low- and semiskilled jobs to men who did not necessarily need high school diplomas to get or perform them. Americanization—the transmission and preservation of traditional Anglo/European culture—was widely accepted and promoted in schools. And legislators were largely oriented toward upholding the status quo. All of this lasted until the 1960s when a postindustrial economic shift took hold and momentous sociocultural transformations took place.

Jobs in the former industrial workplace were outsourced overseas and replaced by new ones that required workers with technical and information management expertise, literacy and computer skills, and other proficiencies requiring higher levels of formal education. Democrats, including President Johnson and many members of Congress, dedicated themselves to ending poverty and a longstanding school achievement gap between low-income Black and middle-class White children. They passed legislation, most notably the 1965 Elementary and Secondary Education Act (ESEA), premised on the assumption that if the cultures of poor Black people were changed poverty would be eliminated and Black student achievement would increase. This assumption, which has not disappeared, is based on the belief that poverty and racial achievement gaps can be lessened through educational programs that compensate for historical disadvantages and cultural deficits.

The economic shift along with notable technological advances propelled a cultural revolution in the 1960s that included a resolute demand for the extension and enforcement of civil rights for Black people and other ethnic minorities, women, and disabled Americans. The movement changed public opinion about the inequitable provision of educational opportunities. Good public schools were now expected to be equally accessible to all children regardless of their race, ethnicity, social class, gender, and special needs. This expectation radically altered judicial, legislative, and political contexts, and ultimately led to the passage of the 1964 Civil Rights Act.

The Civil Rights Act changed U.S. public schools more than any other act in the 20th century. It was instrumental in ending de jure school segregation in the South. The act was followed by a succession of Supreme Court rulings that attempted to dismantle de facto segregation in the North. The rulings spurred White middle-class flight from many urban public high schools as parents concerned about the safety and education of their children moved their families to suburbs or patronized private schools. To make matters worse, inner-city economies were devastated by recessions in the late 1980s that exacerbated joblessness among low-income and working-class men of color. The loss of legitimate employment opportunities encouraged drug trafficking and other illicit enterprises and increased violence and crime rates. These changes had a toxic effect on urban public high schools already reeling from court-ordered desegregation and equal access legislation.

Legislation mandating bilingual education and special education was passed between 1970 and 1990. This legislation was propelled by a noble commitment to make sure all children regardless of their race, ethnicity, social class, language ability, and special needs have equal access to integrated schools and inclusive classrooms with programs that address their individual abilities, interests, and needs. But while this commitment is ideal, it was imposed on urban public high schools so quickly and with so little attention to the realities of life in classrooms and corridors that school cultures and quality instruction were profoundly compromised. Teachers and students were overwhelmed in schools that were overcrowded, blighted with violence, and lacked the resources and support needed to make practical adjustments to economic, social, and cultural changes. Teachers responded by lowering their standards and diminishing their instruction, and students became increasingly alienated from, and resistant to, formal schooling. Dropout rates increased, graduation rates decreased, and overall student learning and achievement plummeted.

An educational accountability movement launched in the 1990s continues to influence policymaking and legislation in the 2000s. Public schools throughout the nation are standardizing curriculum; requiring students to take standardized benchmark and graduation examinations; instituting stricter criteria for teacher licensure; and grading and restructuring public schools on the basis of test scores and other performance indicators. They are also forging partnerships with businesses that have a vested interest in schools that effectively educate students for the workforce.

Other momentous changes resulting from the 1965 immigration reform legislation are also occurring. A growing population of descendents of non-European immigrants is remaking the American mainstream in highly creative ways or, most notably in the case of Islamic conservatives, preserving their traditions in the midst of international conflict.

Despite well-intentioned reform initiatives, urban public high schools continue to be plagued with severe problems that undermine effective pedagogy and harm urban youth. These schools are in dire need of reforms that recognize sociological, cultural, and political facts and insights.

Historical Contexts

Discussion Questions

1. President Johnson and other Democrats waged a war on poverty in the 1960s that included legislation that introduced and funded compensatory education programs. Do you agree with the assumption that school achievement can be improved through educational programs intended to change or compensate for the cultures of poor Black families and other people living in poverty? Why or why not?
2. The Supreme Court issued rulings in the 1970s that included orders for the immediate desegregation of racially segregated school systems. How did these rulings affect urban public high schools? What are their legacies today?
3. The postindustrial economy coupled with a recession in the 1980s led to significant joblessness and a significant rise in violence among inner-city youth, especially young men who belong to racial and ethnic minority groups. How did the loss of legitimate economic opportunities affect urban youths' attitudes toward schooling?
4. The 1990s saw the beginnings of an educational accountability movement which has relied very heavily on standardized testing. Is standardized testing crucial for raising student achievement in urban public high schools? Why or why not?

Note

1. There is an academic debate about whether it is more appropriate to use pan-ethnic categories like *Latino* or *Hispanic* or group identifiers stated in terms of specific national origin (e.g., Puerto Rican, Dominican, Columbian, Ecuadoran, or Peruvian). Kasinitz et al. (2008) conducted a study involving immigrants and their adult children from Central and South America, Puerto Rico, the Dominican Republic, and other Spanish-speaking countries and discovered that they attached varied meanings to the terms *Hispanic*, *Latino*, and *Spanish* and switched back and forth among them and with specific national origin so much that, as far as they were concerned, there is no right or wrong label to use with this population. I use the term *Latino* in this book to collectively refer to these groups *because* of its more widespread usage especially in the Western United States.

2

SOCIOLOGICAL BASICS

School Functions, Social Locations, and Capital

Functions of Schooling

The relationship between schools and society has been a primary interest of sociologists for over a century. As Émile Durkheim (1956) observed long ago, the essential purpose of public schools is to socialize young people into "the community of ideas and sentiments without which any society is impossible ... and the special milieu for which [they are] specifically destined" (p. 53). Talcott Parsons (1959), in his classic article on schooling in American society, explains in a similar vein how schools are social systems structured to function as agencies of socialization into adult roles and allocation into occupational statuses generally associated with bifurcated groups of college-goers and non-college-goers. *Socialization* processes induct young people into dominant societal values, beliefs, and norms, and entail socioemotional separation from families. *Allocation* is accomplished through sorting mechanisms that channel students into educational and occupational tracks. These mechanisms uphold the status quo in ways that reinforce society's hierarchically stratified socioeconomic structure.

In public high school social systems, the stakes for achieving upward mobility through formal education are very high. Adolescent students recognize the importance of schooling and are well aware of the selective processes of allocation. They generally endorse the dominant ritualized educational *regime* with its universal "common script" for what high schools ought to be like in terms of curriculum, class scheduling, and the other ritual classifications that make school actors feel like they are participants in a "real school ... rich with symbols of participation in cultured society and in access to opportunity" (Metz, 1990, p. 83). But they do not necessarily go along with the *regimen* of schooling

---

CONCEPT BOX 2.1

Functions of Schooling

Socialization: Public schools are expected to socialize all students into larger societal values, beliefs, and norms.

Allocation: Public schools are also expected to sort individual students into differentiated educational and occupational tracks.

(distinct from the ritualized educational regime) especially in classrooms where they are expected to follow orders unquestioningly, complete tedious assignments, take difficult tests, and otherwise comply with a teacher-driven system that places unpleasant burdens on them (Hemmings, 2003). Schools' social systems uphold larger societal systems through teachers' regimented transmission of dominant societal understandings and differentiated curriculum and students' willingness to learn what is deliberately taught to them. It is a social system where adult teachers are ultimately dependent on adolescent students to carry out their work effectively (Metz, 1993). The nature and extent to which adolescents go along with their teachers is very much influenced by social class and its intersections with race, ethnicity, gender, sexual orientation, and other social locations.

Social Locations: Class and Intersections with Race, Ethnicity, and Gender

Social class, and the closely related concept of socioeconomic status (SES), is the most statistically predictive variable in formal educational attainments. Simply put, the higher a student's social class the more likely it is that he or she will graduate from high school and acquire postsecondary credentials. There is social stratification in the United States based in part on SES indicators of income, occupation, and educational attainments. Groups with high SES enjoy higher status and more social privilege and power in relation to groups with lower SES. They are exclusive rather than inclusive of those who are perceived as less privileged.

Social class intersects with race, ethnicity, gender, sexual orientation, and other social locations in ways that shape group affiliation, identification, and stratification. There is a wide and fluid range of social groups in the United States comprised of people with distinctive or intertwined social locations. People in these groups share similar social habits, cultural commitments, and modes of communication, discourses, and language codes that convey group affiliation and identity and affect the meanings members attach to themselves, other people, things, events, and other phenomena (Bernstein, 1971; Little-john, 2002). Groups compete with one another for status and other social, cultural, and economic resources that will enable them to occupy the top rungs of the stratified ladder.

Race is an especially important social location in the United States that is constructed on the basis of skin color and other physical attributes. People of color, especially Black Americans, have been subjected to generations of discrimination and prejudice, and ascribed highly pejorative social statuses reinforced by negative stereotypes. People who are regarded as "White" enjoy more privileged social locations. *Ethnicity*, another social location, is comprised of distinctions made on the basis of national origin, language, religion, and other cultural identifiers. It is linked to whether members of an ethnic group are Native Americans, descended from groups who immigrated to the United States long ago, were conquered or arrived as war refugees, or are more recent immigrants or their descendents. *Gender* and *sexual orientation* are social locations defined in terms of physical sexual differences and sexual preferences.

The intersection of these and other social locations with social class has a profound impact on the social mobility of groups as well as the social and educational experiences of students in urban high schools. The ways in which social locations are woven into the social and cultural fabric of groups are highly nuanced and dynamic. They shape and reshape high school students' social identities and behavior; how students are treated and treat others; and how students interact with other individuals and groups. They also affect students' access to, and ability and willingness to expend economic, cultural, social, and symbolic capital.

Economic, Cultural, Social, and Symbolic Capital

Economic, cultural, social, and symbolic capital is critical for educational pursuits. Bourdieu (1977; Bourdieu & Passeron, 1990) and other scholars offer powerful theoretical insights into these forms of capital in education, and how their uneven distribution contributes to the reproduction of socioeconomic inequalities. *Economic capital* is the income, accumulated wealth, and loan credit that people use to purchase high-quality, high-status formal educations. *Cultural capital* includes valued academic and mainstream cultural knowledge and the cultural dispositions most conducive for success in school settings (Brubaker, 2004). It is also derived from the cultural connections people make with books, computers, and other education-related objects as well as universities, libraries, and other education-related institutions (Grenfell & James, 1998; Robbins, 2000). *Social capital* is the social resources and networks that enable people to promote their own or others' educational achievement and attainment. It is acquired through resources both educational (e.g., books, study aids, academic tutoring) and auxiliary (e.g., psychological counseling, substance abuse treat-

---

CONCEPT BOX 2.2

Economic, Cultural, Social, and Symbolic Capital

Economic capital: Income, wealth, and loan credit.

Cultural capital: Personal dispositions, attitudes, cultural knowledge gained from experience, and connections to education-related objects and institutions.

Social capital: Social networks, reciprocity in social relations, and resources such as tutoring, counseling, and legal assistance.

Symbolic capital: Recognition of competence and being competent in various arenas.

---

ment, medical services, legal assistance) and is dispensed through obligations, expectations, and other reciprocal understandings within and between families and schools. Social capital is also acquired by people who are, or become, integrated into dominant social networks in schools and other institutions. It is, in other words, the strategic social means for reaching desirable social ends. *Symbolic capital* is the recognition of competence and being competent in various social areas. It is used in high schools to garner respect and status.

These forms of capital along with organizational and other forces shape the contours of an individual's *habitus* which may be in sync with, or run against the grain of, educational *fields*. Habitus is a system of internalized dispositions for thinking and behaving. It is the rules of the game that people internalize and follow. Fields are structured systems of social relations. Students experience significant social advantages if their habitus is consistent with the fields they encounter in schools (Brubaker, 2004; Lareau, 2001; Reed-Danahay, 2005).

Students are disadvantaged, and likely to resist schooling, if their habitus is not aligned with educational fields. The characteristics of schools' semibureaucratic organization have a profound effect on educational fields and how school actors adjust to them.

CONCEPT BOX 2.3

Habitus and Educational Fields

Habitus: Internalized dispositions for thinking and behaving. It constitutes the rules of the game.

Educational Fields: Structured systems of social relations in schools and other educational settings.

School Semibureaucracy

It has been argued, understandably so, that the most defining characteristic of urban public high schools is their bureaucratic organizational structure (Meyer & Rowan, 1983; Weiner, 1999, 2000). High schools, especially those located in urban districts, are often described as overly bureaucratic in ways that isolate them from communities, intensify the rift between personalized and standardized instruction, and disempower administrators, teachers, students, and parents (Fine, 1994b; Meyer & Zucker, 1989). While such negative effects may very well be attributed to organizational structures, urban high schools, like all schools, are actually distinctly semibureaucratic in their organization (deMarrais & LeCompte, 1999).

Max Weber (1925/1947), a sociologist during the early part of the 20th century, developed the best known if not definitive conceptualization of bureaucracy, which he described in conjunction with notions of rationality. He viewed rational bureaucracies as complex organizations established to meet formal goals through the efficient management of people holding various positions that have specified tasks associated with them. Weber assembled the key characteristics of rational bureaucracies into an "ideal type" that could be used to analyze how organizations actually function. These characteristics include (1) formally stated goals; (2) well defined technologies (work processes); (3) job positions with specified responsibilities, obligations, and rights; (4) an authority structure with systems of supervision and subordination; (5) extensive use of written documents including detailed record keeping; (6) rules and regulations which are clear, consistent, and enforceable; and (7) hiring procedures and work assignments based on individuals' competence and experience. High schools, especially those in urban districts, diverge in notable ways from Weber's ideal type. This is especially true with regards to goals, technologies, structure, and authority.

Goals

In her classic sociological study of two middle schools, Mary Haywood Metz (1978) describes secondary schools' bureaucratic divergences, including those related to goals. While the goals of schooling at the surface level of public perception appear to be clear with widespread consensus about the aims of public education, it becomes apparent upon deeper inspection that educational goals are "endless in their variety and subtle in their complexity" (Metz, 1978, p. 16). When more penetrating questions are asked about what it really means to educate young people, the façade of public agreement crumbles into fierce debates that reach to the highest levels of federal and state policy making and legislation on down into the more localized spheres of communities, school districts, schools, and ultimately classrooms.

The formal goals of schooling are not only endlessly variable and subtle, but they are also contestable and contradictory. Because of this, as Metz goes on to explain, schools have an array of instrumental goals to accomplish perennially ill-defined ends. The most important instrumental goal is the maintenance of order among half-socialized students compelled by law to attend schools and who have "radically different educational and social expectations" (Metz, 1978, p. 17). Instrumental goals are essential but they are not necessarily conducive to the fulfillment of educational goals (whatever they happen to be). They can change or subvert educational goals, and often take precedence over the ideal ends of teaching and learning. This is especially likely to occur in urban public high schools where low-income, historically marginalized, racial and ethnic minority students may be disaffected to the point where they feel like, and may in effect be, inmates in a prisonlike regimen intended to keep them under orderly control.

Technologies

Metz (1978) also explicates the uncertainties of school technologies and the difficulties of defining and applying ones that are universally effective and reliable. Technologies are the work processes that an organization adopts to transform raw material (e.g. inanimate matter, people, or symbols) into outcomes tied to

---

CONCEPT BOX 2.4

Characteristics of Semibureaucratic School Organization

Goals: Formal educational goals are variable, contestable, and contradictory. Instrumental goals are necessary for maintaining order but may subvert formal goals.

Technologies (work processes): Technologies are uncertain. Not possible to determine if instructional technologies are effective in long run or that one approach is more superior or reliable than another.

Structure: Ritualized classification structures (e.g., credentialing, class schedules, curricular topics, guidelines, and standards, graduation requirements) are tightly coupled and controlled at every level. Activity structures are loosely coupled with some autonomy and depend on logic of confidence (trust) between levels. Tracking structures sort students into classes with differentiated curriculum and vary in nature, meanings, and practices within and between schools.

Authority: Authority relations are unstable. Teachers must assert their dominance over students with no assurances of compliance.

formal goals. Chief among the technologies in schools are those used by teachers in classrooms to instruct, assess, and control students. Students as raw material are highly variable in terms of their cultural background, social position, and emotional and cognitive characteristics. They make it virtually impossible for teachers to come up with a well-defined set of classroom technologies that work in all instances with all students all of the time. To complicate matters, there is no way to know for sure if an approach is effective for the long run, or one technology is better than another. Classroom technologies are endemically uncertain.

Structure

Ritual Classification and Activity Structures.
High schools also diverge from the rational bureaucratic ideal type in terms of their structure. In organizations that are more purely bureaucratic in their operations, structures are centralized and hierarchical and decision making is top-down. Upper levels of the structure are tightly coupled to lower levels through procedures and direct inspections intended to ensure that work at all levels is being carried out efficiently and effectively. In public high schools, ritual classification structures are tightly controlled especially with regards to credentialing, class schedules, curricular topics, guidelines, and standards, graduation requirements, and other "societally agreed-on rites defined in societal myths (institutional rules) of education" (Meyer & Rowan, 1983, p. 65). But activity structures, what actually happens in classrooms, offices, and other school spaces, are loosely coupled. Educational work takes place in isolated spaces that are usually quite removed from the types of direct procedural controls and inspections characterizing rational bureaucracies (Weick, 1983). Activity structures depend on a "logic of confidence" where people occupying higher levels assume that what is going on at lower levels makes sense and conforms to institutional rules (societal rites and myths of education) in ways that avoid direct oversight, which in most public schools is practically impossible (Meyer & Rowan, 1983):

> Interaction in school systems … is characterized both by the assumption of good faith and the actualities of decoupling. This is the logic of confidence: Parties bring to each other the taken-for-granted, good-faith assumption that the other is, in fact, carrying out his or her defined activity. The community and board have confidence in the superintendent, who has confidence in the principal, who has confidence in the teachers. None of these people can say what the other does or produces, but the plausibility of their activity requires that they have confidence in each other. (p. 79)

The structure of work activities is, in other words, based on trust. Everybody trusts everyone else to do their jobs without anyone paying close attention to what anyone is actually doing.

A practical reason for the loose coupling of activity structures is the uncertainty of technologies. It is not feasible for upper-level school officials to coordinate and control lower-level classroom teachers because there is no one right or clear way to teach and maintain control over students. Direct inspection of teaching is sporadic and can be rare especially in urban high schools where administrators are overwhelmed with other responsibilities.

One way to exert tighter control over teaching is through inspection of outputs such as results on standardized tests. The passage of No Child Left Behind legislation has spurred the institutionalization of this form of accountability through high-stakes testing mechanisms that in many districts are being used to monitor and evaluate teachers' performance. But there has been a great deal of resistance to the idea of using student achievement data to control the work of teachers because they do not guarantee that students will perform their jobs as learners. Many students, especially those in urban public high schools, feel they have nothing to gain, or lose, if they do poorly on standardized tests. They cannot get fired, docked in pay, or otherwise sanctioned like bottom-of-the-rung workers in other organizations.

Tracking Structures.   Another common high school structure is academic and vocational tracking. Academic tracking is a process whereby students are categorized as fast, average, or slow learners on the basis of test scores and past performance and then placed into lower-level (e.g., special education and remedial), regular-level, or upper-level (e.g., honors and Advanced Placement) classes (Oakes, 1985). Vocational tracking offers programs geared toward postsecondary occupations that do not require college credentials. Tracking is supposed to involve fair placements based on students' innate abilities and personal aspirations. But some view it as profoundly unfair and directly implicated in the reproduction of society's unequal socioeconomic structure. Neo-Marxist reproduction theorists, prominent in the 1970s and 80s, took note of how disproportionate numbers of low-income, racial and ethnic minority students are placed in the lowest rungs of the academic and vocational tracks while White, European American, middle-class students are overrepresented in upper-level classes (Bowles & Gintis, 1976). They claim that students in lower-track classes are taught lower-status knowledge and subjected to strict disciplinary controls in preparation for working- and lower-class jobs while those in the upper tracks are provided with high-status knowledge and skills and given more freedom to express themselves. There is, in other words, a correspondence between the structure of high school tracking and the unequally stratified socioeconomic structure of society.

But the correspondence is neither clear cut nor uniform across urban high schools. There is significant variation within and between schools regarding the nature and meanings associated with different tracks and the curriculum, instruction, and disciplinary practices that characterize them (Page & Valli,

1990). Lower- and upper-track classes in urban high schools serving low-income, heterogeneous student populations are qualitatively different from, and may parody, ones in more demographically homogeneous, middle-class districts (Metz, 1990; Page, 1990). Context matters and matters enormously in how tracking is structured locally as well as in relation to larger societal structures.

Authority

Authority is another organizational feature, which Metz (1978) defines as:

> the right of a person in a specified role to give commands to which a person in another specified role has a duty to render obedience. This right and duty rest upon the superordinate's recognized status as the legitimate representative of a moral order to which both superordinate and subordinate owe allegiance. (p. 27)

Authority is an institutional relationship between superordinates and subordinates which is, strictly speaking, more of a relationship of roles rather than of persons. The role of superordinates is to issue commands and provide direction with the presumption that they have the ability to meet the needs of the organization's moral order. The moral order, described below in more detail, is a set of shared understandings and practices that hold organizational actors together and guide the proper or right way to realize goals (Selznick, 1992). The authority of the superordinate depends upon his or her legitimate claim to be acting on behalf of the moral order. The role of subordinates is to follow superordinates' commands and directions also in allegiance to the moral order.

There are different types of authority that teachers may exercise including traditional, charismatic, legal–rational, professional, and moral authority (Pace & Hemmings, 2006b, 2006c, 2007; Weber 1925/1947). *Traditional authority* is based on established beliefs that grant legitimacy to those in superordinate positions. Teachers exercising this type of authority uphold the time-honored conventions of formal schooling. Those with *charismatic authority* evoke emotional attachment and enjoy unusually high prestige. They are not bound by rules or conventions and inspire students with their contagious passion and commitment. Teachers utilizing *legal–rational authority* (also known as bureaucratic authority) essentially enact the role of boss in classroom workplaces. Their authority is supported by rules and policies that include the right to use rewards and punishments to enforce commands. *Professional authority* rests on individual expertise (Blau, 1974; Parsons, 1947). Teachers with professional authority assert themselves as experts with a strong command of subject matter and knowledge (Grant, 1988; Metz, 1978; Pace, 2003a, 2006). Durkheim (1956) emphasizes the importance of teachers' *moral authority* as an "influence which imposes upon us all the moral power that we acknowledge as superior to us" (p. 29).

Despite this repertoire of authority types, many K–12 teachers experience difficulties in establishing and maintaining authority in their relations with students. Authority relations in schools are inherently unstable. Schools, sociologist Willard Waller (1932/1961) observes, are "despotisms in a state of perilous equilibrium" where teachers must assert their dominance before teaching can occur and where students are prone to be antagonistic towards classroom regimens (p. 10). Classroom authority relations exist in a "quivering" balance that may be upset at any moment (p. 383). A teacher's dominance cannot be assured in classrooms where conflict and student resistance lie constantly in wait ready to erupt (Pace & Hemmings, 2006c, 2007). Authority relations are especially unstable in urban public high schools where socially and economically marginalized students may not be entirely convinced that compliance with classroom regimens will lead to gainful postsecondary educational and occupational opportunities (Giroux, 1983; Willis, 1977).

Because of schools' semibureaucratic activity structure, teachers are pretty much on their own with regard to whether or how they will establish their authority. While teachers have a fair amount of autonomy to try out different strategies, the structure does not guarantee that they will have authority in their relations with students. The situation is complicated by the constraints that are placed on teachers by the more tightly coupled ritualized classifications of credentialing, class schedules, graduation requirements, curricular topics, guidelines, and standards, and also through accountability mechanisms such as high-stakes testing. School culture is especially critical in systems like this because of how it can bind and guide school actors or divide and confound them.

School Organizational Culture and Subcultures

Organizational Culture of Schools

School organizational cultures have the most fundamental and potent ground-level impact on how educational processes are actually enacted in urban public high schools. They have been defined as the patterns of norms, values, practices, beliefs, and other meanings that guide the thoughts and behaviors of organizational actors (Kuh & Whitt, 1998); moral orders to which people owe allegiance in fulfillment of organizational goals (Selznick, 1992); behavioral and programmatic regularities and patterns that govern roles and interrelationships and define the permissible ways in which goals and problems are approached (Sarason, 1996); the *habitus*, or rules of the game, for organizational actions and interactions (Bourdieu & Passeron, 1990; Slater, 1996); frames of reference for individuals and groups to interpret the meanings of events, actions, and things (Kuh & Whitt, 1998); and understandings regarding organizational identities, status, and power that people translate into beliefs about what is possible and not possible for them to do within their particular roles (Slater, 1996).

CONCEPT BOX 2.5

School Organizational Culture

School organizational cultures are comprised of understandings that influence how school actors define their roles, form organizational identities, and render formal schooling into meaningful and actionable practices. Understandings are social constructions produced by school actors during the course of their ongoing interactions. They are negotiable.

These definitions can be boiled down into a basic characterization of school culture as essentially comprised of the understandings with the most direct influence on how school actors define their roles, form organizational identities, and render formal schooling into meaningful and actionable practices. While public high schools are similar in terms of scripted ritual classifications (e.g., class offerings, scheduling, curriculum topics, guidelines, and standards, graduation requirements), they have significantly different cultural modes for the performance of roles, adoption of practices, and other patterns ultimately characterizing everyday organizational life because of the highly localized constellations of understandings that emerge within them (Page & Valli, 1990). No two high school organizational cultures are alike even though they are subject to common scripts for schooling.

School organizational cultures are often rife with paradoxical understandings which are especially consequential for moral orders most closely associated with the fulfillment of educational goals. These orders have moral overtones of right and wrong that affect the meanings of "worthwhile" curriculum, "proper" leadership and pedagogy, "good" character, and other features of schooling that have a profound impact on what "should" or "ought" to happen in administrative offices, classrooms, and corridors (Hemmings, 2006a). When paradoxical understandings are infused into these meanings, counteracting approaches to schooling inevitably arise.

Such was the case in a Midwestern urban public high school serving Black students from low-income families (Hemmings, 2004, 2006a). The school's moral order had an enabling communitarian ethic of care that was paradoxically juxtaposed against a disenabling lack of care for student learning. Teachers listened to students' personal problems and provided whatever help they could, but they also trivialized curriculum, assigned mindless seatwork, and otherwise watered down valuable academic knowledge and skills. They cared for Black youths in dire need of emotional, physical, and other assistance, but did not care about making sure Black students received a good education.

Social Construction of School Organizational Culture

The actual nature of school organizational cultures and the moral orders embedded in them depends on how they are constructed by school actors during the course of their ongoing social relations. Patterns or regularities in administrative operations, classroom regimens, and corridor student life arise in all high schools and are upheld to the extent that the people who construct them sustain them. They are not constructed solely in situ, but reflect broader historical and sociocultural understandings (Page & Valli, 1990). School actors produce them within the restrictive constraints, and autonomous spaces, that characterize schools' semibureaucratic structures. But their constructions are also affected by national, state, and local community pressures.

The concept of socially constructed patterns has its sociological roots in the work of Berger and Luckmann (1967) who emphasize the importance of commonsense knowledge as the "fabric of meanings," or subjective reality that people weave together during their social interactions (p. 15). Blumer (1969) explains the social construction process, which he terms *symbolic interactionism,* as resting on three basic premises:

> The first premise is that human beings act toward things on the basis of the meanings that the things have for them.... The second premise is that the meaning of such things is derived from, or arises out of, the social interaction that one has with one's fellows. The third premise is that these meanings are handled in, and modified through, an interpretive process used by the person in dealing with the things he encounters. (p. 1)

People define the social situations they are in during the course of their interactions. Their definitions constitute the situation-specific understandings that inform their behaviors. These understandings may be maintained over-time or they may be modified, discarded, or invented as situations change and people come and go. The particular actions that individuals take are adopted and enacted during these symbolic interactions. The rules governing actions are not rigid but, rather, subject to reinforcement or alterations as meanings are constructed and reconstructed.

There is a great deal of relational work in the social construction of organizational cultural understandings that informs what happens in administrative offices, classrooms, and corridors. The significance of this sociological perspective for urban public high schools is that the understandings that inform situational behaviors are fluid, negotiable, and constantly contested. They depend on the dynamics of administrator–teacher, teacher–student, and student–student relations, which are very much shaped by subcultures.

Teacher Subcultures

All schools have subcultures where general organizational understandings, including paradoxical ones, are translated into more nuanced meanings in light of group interests, individual convictions, external pressures, and other factors. Faculty subcultures are especially significant because of their direct effects on how teachers view their roles, form professional identities, choose and justify their practices, and judge students. They can be divided along subject areas, years of service, pedagogical philosophies, and other lines, and they run the gamut from peaceful coexistence to heated conflict.

Teachers become clannish and sometimes combative when subcultural cleavages are severe. Metz (1978) observed two bitterly opposed factions in a school where faculty members were split between those embracing a whole-child developmental approach and those upholding an incorporative philosophy where teacher-centered methods designed to incorporate knowledge into students were strongly endorsed. Resentment between factions was so intense that each group staked out different territories in the faculty lounge with virtually no lines of communication between them. Students picked up on the split, had no reason to believe one approach was better than another, and expressed their own preferences in an environment where there were no universal or consistent responses to their behavior. Teachers were so deeply divided that there was no unified effort to prevent students from unsettling the culture even more.

A particularly insidious element in faculty subcultures is how different groups of students come to be judged as morally acceptable or unacceptable. Low-income racial and ethnic minority students, especially those prone to resistance, may be pegged as unacceptable and "morally tainted with the values of … illegitimate community lifestyle[s]" (Metz, 1993, p. 132). The belief that these youths are deficient is rampant in many urban public high schools, and faculty subcultures reinforce or counteract it with obvious consequences for students. Some groups dismiss students as unworthy, unteachable, and not worth the effort. Others attempt to compensate for perceived deficits through simplified or remedial instruction. Still others reject the notion of student deficits as "blaming the victim" and deploy heroic means to lead their classes to more socially and academically uplifting ends (Weiner, 1999). Students spin their own youth cultures and subcultures in reaction to the signals they receive from teachers and also to other powerful influences.

Youth Cultures and Student Peer-Group Subcultures

Youth cultures and more localized student peer-group subcultures have a profound impact on whether and how teenagers comply with schooling regimens. Talcott Parsons (1964) originally coined the phrase *youth culture* to refer to the distinctive patterns of behaviors that adolescents express during the transitional phase between childhood dependence and adult independence. Sociologists in the 1960s characterized these behaviors as deviant if they strayed too far from middle-class work expectations and social sensibilities. This interpretation was modified in the 1970s by neo-Marxists, especially those associated with Britain's Birmingham School, who emphasized the class-based origins of youth cultures rooted in alienation among working-class youths confronting seemingly insurmountable structural barriers to socioeconomic mobility (Brake, 1980, 1985; Cohen, 1980; Epstein, 1998). Paul Willis (1977) conducted what became a classic study of working-class boys in an English high school who adopted an antischool youth counterculture laced with the macho, shop-floor values of their fathers. They made fun of schooling, and the classmates who took schooling seriously, because they did not believe it would pay off for them.

A subsequent proliferation of resistance theories rendered the concept of youth culture into understandable if not justifiable responses to an unjust social order. Some, like John Ogbu and his adherents, focused on race and ethnicity and how perceived job ceilings cause African Americans, Latinos, and other involuntary minority high school students to defy White domination through oppositional cultural frames of reference and collective identities (Fordham, 1988, 1996, 2008; Fordham & Ogbu, 1986; Matute-Bianchi, 1991; Ogbu, 1978, 1987; Ogbu & Simons, 1998). These youths resist schooling because accommodation is regarded as "acting White" and therefore inappropriate for them. Other scholars, such as Nancy Lesko (1988) examined gendered resistance. Lesko observed girls in a Catholic high school opposing self-restrictive images of the good girl with bold expressions of dirty language, provocative dress, and outright insubordination.

Many of these students are under the influence of popular culture marketed to them through videos, movies, CDs, and other media. They weave this material into youth culture and peer subcultures in ways that can reinforce negative racial and ethnic stereotypes, sexist treatment of women, illegal drug use, violence, and intergroup hostilities (Giroux, 1998; Hemmings, 2002). The infusion of popular culture into youth culture and subcultures has a socially symbolic and profoundly potent influence on expressions of student resistance.

Although studies have shown resistance to schooling is common among historically marginalized urban high school students, findings also indicate that students' expressions are inconsistent. High school students are constantly positioning and repositioning themselves through fluid adaptations, especially those constructed and expressed within peer-group subcultures (Davidson, 1996; Hemmings, 2002; Weis & Fine, 2000). Subcultures reinforce, modify, or counteract racial, classed, and gendered images of urban youth in ways that shape students' academic identities and willingness to comply with teachers' directions. Students constantly fluctuate between resistance and accommodation or some blend of the extremes in their social maneuverings within and between classroom and corridors. They engage in social constructions of cultural expressions in their social relations.

Summation

Urban high schools, from a basic sociological point of view, are places where adolescents are socialized into society's dominant values, beliefs, and norms, and allocated into adult occupational roles. They are semibureaucratic organizations with variable and contested goals; uncertain technologies; tightly coupled ritual classifications and loosely coupled activity structures; and unstable authority relations. A significant number of these schools enroll large numbers of racial and ethnic minority youths many of whom are from low-income and working-class families. There is a strong correlation between students' social class and formal educational attainments. Social class intersects with race, ethnicity, gender, and other social locations in ways that influence students' willingness to accommodate to, or resist, formal schooling.

Whether or how students engage in schooling processes is also affected by their access to, or willingness to expend, crucial economic, cultural, social, and symbolic capital. These forms of capital shape the contours of habitus—systems of internalized thinking and behaving—that may or may not be in sync with the structured systems of social relations comprising educational fields, with profound consequences for school success.

Urban high schools are characterized by organizational cultures comprised of the most fundamental understandings that define the roles, identities, and behaviors of administrators, teachers, students, and other school actors. These cultures are social constructions created, dismantled, revived, or otherwise produced during the course of social relations. They have moral orders tied to goals that are often rife with paradoxical understandings about what should be happening in offices, classrooms, and corridors. There are also teacher and student subcultures with more nuanced understandings produced in light of group interests, individual convictions, external pressures, and other factors. Teacher subcultures affect the ways in which different groups of teachers view their roles, form professional identities, choose and justify their practices, and judge students. They can fuel conflict between faculty cliques or pull faculty together. And they influence teachers' perceptions of students as morally acceptable or unworthy of their time and effort.

Student youth cultures and subcultures heavily influenced by popular culture are symbolic assertions of individual and group identity and adolescent independence. They can incite resistance to schooling, encourage compliance, or play into contradictory adaptations as students work to position and reposition themselves during the course of their social interactions with peers and teachers. Teachers in their work are ultimately dependent on students who are well aware of, and deliberately reactive to, their social status and power in relation to others.

Sociological Basics

Discussion Questions

1. There is widespread support in the United States for a universal public school regime with ritualized common scripts for schooling. But high school students, especially those in urban districts, do not necessarily go along with the regimens of schooling. From a sociological point of view, why are low-income and working-class students in urban high schools prone to resist regimented classroom instruction?
2. People in the United States do not have the same access to the economic, cultural, social, and symbolic capital that procures advantages in educational and occupational pursuits. How might such capital be distributed in urban public high schools that serve large numbers of low-income and working-class racial and ethnic minority students?
3. Urban public high schools are semibureaucratic organizations with contested goals, uncertain technologies, tightly and loosely coupled structures, and unstable authority relations. Should these schools be more purely bureaucratic with clear goals and certain technologies, tightly coupled structures, and procedures that ensure student compliance? Why or why not?
4. Urban high school organizational cultures and subcultures are constructed by students, teachers, administrators, and staff during ongoing relations that may be riddled with intergroup social conflict. How might social conflict in urban high schools be mediated so that school actors can work together to construct organizational cultures that promote educational and occupational opportunities?

3

ANTHROPOLOGICAL PERSPECTIVES

Cultural Processes in Urban High Schools

Anthropologists study culture as essentially the "patterns *for* behavior and patterns *of* behavior" that are adopted by people in various social groups (Jacob & Jordan, 1993, p. 15). Swidler (1986) defines culture in more analytical detail as symbolic forms of meaning that include formalized beliefs, ritual practices, art forms, and ceremonies, as well as informal practices such as language and those that pervade daily routines. These forms are cultural tool kits that people use and configure in various ways in their solutions to the perennial problems of human existence, especially those related to reproduction, birth, maturation, and death, as well as the more mundane exigencies of everyday life. They coalesce into strategies of action adopted by groups where there are regular, ongoing interactions. Group members utilize these strategies in their adaptations which may be modified or abandoned depending on the circumstances.

Whereas sociologists of education are primarily concerned with school organizational culture, which was defined in chapter 2 as the understandings that influence how school actors define their roles, form organizational identities, and render formal schooling into meaningful and actionable practices, educational anthropologists study culture as symbolic forms that inform ways of community life and individual lifestyles. They view the cultural milieu of public schools as reaffirmations of Anglo/European, middle-class cultural commitments. This milieu is reflected in an academic curriculum deeply ensconced in Anglo/European literature, science, music, history, mathematics, and other literary, artistic, and scholarly works. Standard American English is the official school lingua franca and foreign language offerings generally include Spanish, French, German, and other European languages. There are also a number of rituals, holiday celebrations, and extracurricular clubs, sports, and activities

CONCEPT BOX 3.1

Definition of Culture

Cultures are comprised of symbolic forms of meaning that include formalized beliefs, ritual practices, art forms, and ceremonies, as well as informal practices such as language and daily routines. These forms constitute tool kits that people configure into solutions to perennial human problems and the handling of everyday life exigencies. They coalesce within groups into patterned strategies of action.

imbued with the milieu. And while there has been an effort in recent years to acknowledge other cultural contributions in curriculum and extracurricular events, Anglo/European, middle-class culture is, and has always been, the dominant ethos in U.S. public high schools.

Urban high schools are expected to transmit this way of life as the common national or mainstream culture. Such transmission occurs through *enculturation,* which in school settings is a process where students become competent in the surrounding mainstream culture. Schools also promote processes of *acculturation,* which occurs in situations where people embracing different cultures find themselves in continuous contact, and as a result of their interactions change or sustain their original cultural patterns. They accommodate to the cultural adjustments that come about through the intermingling of students from different cultural backgrounds.

Cultural identity work has a profound impact on how and to what extent racially and ethnically diverse high school students accommodate to dominant cultural systems. It involves the formation and performance of academic identities against the backdrop of what it means to be an educated person.

CONCEPT BOX 3.2

Enculturation and Acculturation

Enculturation: Process where people become culturally competent by learning the symbolic forms of the surrounding culture.

Acculturation: Process where people embrace different cultures and as a result of continuous contact change or sustain their original cultural patterns.

Cultural Identity Work

Self, External Cultural Pressures, and Identity Work

Adolescence in the human development lifespan is a period of intense identity formation. Teenagers, according to Yon (2000), have a

> passion for identities … made around nation, community, ethnicity, race, religion, gender, sexuality, and age; identities premised on popular culture and its shifting sets of representational practices; identities attached to fashion and new imagined lifestyles, to leisure and work, and to the mundane and the exotic; identities made in relation to place and displacement, to community and to a sense of dispersal, to "roots" as well as "routes." (p. 1)

Educational anthropologists have long understood the essential importance of the cultural identity work of high school students because identity provides youths with a rationale for the actions they take, and helps to explain why they do what they do (Staiger, 2006). Adolescent identity formation is studied as something "made" around nation, community, ethnicity, race, religion, gender, sexuality, and age. Identity work is connected to processes of enculturation and cultural transmission with close attention to what it means to become a person in a particular cultural context.

Diane Hoffman (1998), in her conceptualization of cultural identity, provides keen insight into the relationship between the innermost self and external cultural pressures. The innermost self is comprised of individuals' most deeply ingrained psychocultural commitments, which include psychological orientations and culturally patterned ways of "relating to others; to the material, natural, and spiritual worlds; and to time and space, including notions of agency, mind, person, being and spirit" (Hoffman, 1998, p. 326). External cultural pressures emanate from the cultural systems produced and promoted within families, neighborhoods, schools, and other groups, places, and institutions. Shweder (1991) refers to these systems as "intentional worlds" because their cultural "scheme of things," or systems, are comprised of knowledge, norms, values, and other meanings intended to script inhabitants' self and behaviors as well as their relations with others (p. 74). Adolescents' intentional worlds are not necessarily characterized by the same cultural scripts nor are scripts always embraced by all inhabitants. These worlds often convey conflicting messages that teenagers respond to as "intentional persons" who actively absorb, mediate, contest, or transform them.

George and Louise Spindler (1992, 1993) provide a more nuanced view of the interplay between the innermost self and external cultural pressures. The *enduring self,* their term for deeply ingrained psychocultural commitments, is not a unified and stable whole, but rather, a multifaceted, somewhat fragmented set

---

CONCEPT BOX 3.3

Self and Cultural Identity Work

Enduring Self: Innermost psychocultural commitments.

Situated Self: Outward expressions of understandings of cultural meanings pertaining to what activities are linked to what goals as well as how to behave to reach desired ends. It involves demonstrations of cultural competence.

Endangered Self: Risks to the self that arise when cultural pressures conflict with group cultural commitments or threaten psychological well-being.

Cultural Identity Work: Adaptations to cultural pressures within and between intentional worlds that enable people to be true to their enduring selves; function effectively in different cultural contexts; and lessen the risks of self-endangerment.

---

of commitments that evolves as individuals mature and circumstances change. Despite its fluidity, the enduring self provides people with a sense of continuity with the past and a compass of meanings for navigating the present and charting the future.

The *situated self* is the outward expression of individuals' understanding of cultural meanings, especially those pertaining to what activities are linked to what goals and ways of behaving in order to reach desired ends. It is instrumental in that it involves practical, outward demonstrations of cultural competence. These demonstrations shift from situation to situation as individuals adapt to different cultural scripts. They may be boldly displayed in one context and carefully suppressed in another.

Attempts to situate the self may go smoothly or lead to intense internal or social conflict. If the enduring self is violated too often by the cultural demands of a situation, it becomes an *endangered self* which can carry real risks for individuals in contexts where cultural pressures conflict with group cultural commitments or threaten their psychological well-being.

Adolescent *cultural identity work* is a process where teenagers actively adapt to external cultural pressures within and between the intentional worlds of their families, schools, peer groups, and other settings in ways that are ideally true to their enduring selves; allow them to function effectively in different cultural contexts; and lessen the risks of self-endangerment. This work can be especially challenging for students in urban schools where there is a vast array of conflicting pressures, which include those associated with what it means to be an educated person in the United States.

The Educated Person, Academic Identity, and Model Student Characteristics

All societies have culturally specific somewhat relative definitions of the educated person. "Distinct societies," Levinson and Holland (1996) explain, "as well as ethnic groups and microcultures within those societies, elaborate the cultural practices by which particular sets of skills, knowledge, and discourses come to define the fully 'educated' person" (p. 2). Each society provides some kind of training in light of cultural criteria by which members are identified as more, or less, educated.

Criteria for the educated person in U.S. schools may affirm the cultures of ethnic minority groups. Trujillo (1996) writes about how teachers in a South Texas town during the course of Chicano civil rights activity developed a pedagogical ideology aimed at creating "a subject-position for a Chicano/a 'educated person,' specifically as a bilingual, culturally proud, communally oriented individual" (p. 144). But such affirmations are not the norm in most urban public high schools where the emphasis is almost always on Anglo/European, middle-class notions of what it means to be fully educated.

Teenagers in the United States who aspire to become educated people usually have a strong *academic identity* where they self-identify with formal schooling and the occupations and lifestyles associated with educational credentialing. They express their identification through an array of strategic accommodations to dominant mainstream school cultural codes and by making an effort to master the curricular knowledge, academic skills, intellectual discourses, and other cultural material, practices, and mindsets they need to demonstrate appropriate cultural competence. They conform in different ways, and to varying degrees to the "model student" image that I found during an ethnographic study of African American high achievers, is comprised of widely recognized characteristics (Hemmings, 1996). Model students are:

CONCEPT BOX 3.4

Educated Person and Academic Identity

Educated Person: Cultural criteria for defining the skills, knowledge, discourses, and other attributes of what it means to be, and be identified as, a fully educated person.

Academic Identity: Self-identification with formal schooling expressed though accommodations to mainstream school cultural codes and efforts to master curricular knowledge, academic skills, intellectual discourse, and other cultural material, practices, and mindsets needed to demonstrate cultural competence as an educated person.

---

1. *Able learners.* They possess the innate ability and academic background necessary for learning grade-level curriculum;
2. *Willing learners.* They have a genuine interest in the curriculum, and complete assignments well and on time;
3. *Solitary learners.* They master curricular content with little or no outside assistance;
4. *Intellectually aggressive.* They show off what they know and are adept at applying mainstream academic epistemologies in scholarly or artistic activities;
5. *Deferential to school authorities.* They are courteous, follow formal rules, and obey the dictates of administrators and teachers;
6. *Culturally mainstream.* They adopt the language, styles of discourse, values, mannerisms, and aesthetic tastes associated with middle-class society and professionals;
7. *College bound.* They compete for good grades, enroll in advanced classes, earn high scores on standardized tests, and otherwise take the steps necessary to meet college admission requirements.

The model student image has been stereotypically associated with some ethnic groups such as Asian Americans (Li & Wang, 2008). But a closer examination of whether or how students from different groups form academic identities as educated people, and perform these identities as model students, reveals much more complex adaptations that are very much affected by the dynamics of cultural differences and conflict in intergroup relations.

Cultural dynamics have a direct bearing on academic achievement patterns, especially on whether and how students adapt to mainstream schooling. Students' responses to the cultural demands of schooling not only affect educational outcomes, but also have a profound often deleterious impact on life in classrooms and corridors. Working-class and low-income racial and ethnic minority students, especially those attending urban high schools, are much more likely to resist schooling than middle-class Anglo/European students and thus fall behind academically. Resistance leads to tensions between students and teachers in classroom situations that can be quite painful and educationally counterproductive. Understanding how cultural processes affect urban high school student academic achievement is therefore of critical importance.

Cultural Theories of Student Achievement

Cultural Deficit Theory

High school academic achievement gaps, which are especially pronounced in urban public high schools serving racial or minority ethnic groups, have existed for decades. Simply stated, middle-class Anglo/European students, Asians, and Jewish Americans have consistently outperformed working-class and low-income African Americans, American Indians, and Latinos. There has been a procession of cultural theories that attempt to explain the gaps beginning with deficit theories that were prevalent, and quite influential, in the 1960s and 1970s. These theories are based on the presupposition that underachieving racial and ethnic minority children are literally deficient in language skills, social development, intellectual competencies, and other areas needed to succeed in school. Cultural deficiencies were theorized as particularly acute among low-income Black children who were presumed to be growing up in families immured in a culture of poverty with value systems that were socially and economically debilitating. Baratz and Baratz (1970) found that the homes of Black and low-income children were being characterized in research and policy circles as "sick, pathological, deviant, or underdeveloped" (p. 29). Such views, Ryan (1972) pointed out, effectively "blamed the victim," children and their families, rather than schools for academic failure and underachievement. The problem was not culturally deprived children but, rather, "culturally depriving schools" (Ryan, 1972, p. 61).

Despite the critiques, the culture of poverty thesis and related cultural deficit theories held sway. They lent support to federal educational policies that led to the introduction of "compensatory" education programs, including Head Start for preschool children and Upward Bound for high school students, aimed at providing low-income children and youth with the skills they presumably lacked to compete in school. The hope was that such programs would eliminate poverty in a generation. But while they have provided many young people with services they might not otherwise have had, they have not closed the gaps between economically disadvantaged students and their middle-class counterparts (Vinovskis, 2009).

Several educational anthropologists took the position that it was not low-income racial and ethnic minority students who were lacking, but rather that deficit theories lacked an understanding of the cultural worlds of schools. They attempted to fill the void with new theories that focused on home–school cultural discontinuities.

Home–School Cultural Discontinuity Theory

Educational anthropologists were among the first to challenge the assumption that racial and ethnic minority groups were somehow deficient in culture. All cultures, they insisted, are rich in language, values, norms, and other meanings and practices, and should be equally valued rather than judged as superior or inferior. In the 1980s the theoretical emphasis was shifted away from cultural deficits within homes to cultural discontinuities between homes and schools. They conceived the home cultures of many racial and ethnic minority groups as somewhat bounded worlds that could be quite different from, or in conflict with, the mainstream cultural worlds affirmed and transmitted in public schools.

Theories focusing on home–school cultural discontinuities were generated based on the premise that the cultural patterns racial and ethnic minority children develop at home with regards to learning, communication, and literary and writing styles may be quite different from teachers' expectations and can provoke problematic classroom interactions (Au, 1980; Delgado-Gaitan, 1987; Erickson & Mohatt, 1982; Heath, 1983; Philips, 1983). Misunderstandings caused by home–school cultural discontinuities may escalate over time and ultimately lead to academic trouble and failure (Erickson, 1987). Racial and ethnic minority children and youths are often portrayed in this work as essentially caught between the two worlds of their homes and schools. They may confront an extremely painful choice between rejecting school in order to stay true to their communities, or leaving their home worlds, sometimes literally, and assimilating into the world of their schools (Rodriguez, 1982).

Many anthropologists who embrace this theoretical perspective recommend forms of culturally responsive teaching that bridge cultural discontinuities in ways that affirm students' home or natal cultures *and* transmit mainstream school culture (Trueba, 1988; Trueba, Spindler, & Spindler, 1988). Culturally responsive teachers essentially teach their students how to code switch; that is, switch from one set of cultural expectations to another as they move between worlds. Students learn how to be bicultural.

The problem with this theoretical approach and corresponding teaching strategies is that many urban public high schools serve multiple racial and ethnic groups characterized by flexible cultural variations within as well as between them. Very few urban youths are growing up in culturally insular homes. And how their home cultures can be affirmed in classrooms where curricular mandates and instructional demands are not readily conducive for culturally responsive teaching is also problematic. Theorists in the new cultural pluralism take explorations of these and other issues a step further.

New Cultural Pluralism Theories

Other theories grouped under the heading of cultural pluralism consider cultural diversity as intrinsic to, and vital for, democracy (Davidson & Phelan, 1993; Newman, 1973; Pai, 1990). Classic versions prevalent in the 1970s characterized societies like the United States as patchworks of bounded ethnic communities with distinctive, viable, and equally valuable cultural traditions. Theorists advanced the claim that members of ethnic communities suffer enormous psychological harm or serious socioeconomic setbacks when their traditions are disrupted through conquest or forced assimilation into another way of life. The integrity of ethnic cultures, they insisted, needs to be preserved through legal protections that, among other guarantees, uphold the right of ethnic groups to control the education of their children.

This theoretical line of thought evolved over time into the "new" cultural pluralism which places more emphasis on the critical relationship between cultural diversity and social stratification in an era of increasing urbanization (Appleton, 1983; Davidson & Phelan, 1993; Hemmings, 1998). Racial and ethnic groups are no longer conceived as bounded communities whose members practice relatively stable ways of life. Communities have flexible cultural systems that may retain long-held ethnic traditions, but also include dominant cultural elements that constantly change through intergroup appropriations, resistances, and accommodations (Marcus & Fischer, 1986). The new cultural pluralism recognizes social conflict as a catalyst for cultural conflict. Increasing urbanization coupled with the explosion of electronic media has intensified contact between previously isolated racial and ethnic communities. Such contact has broken down physical and symbolic barriers between groups, and has led to widespread behavioral assimilation into dominant cultural patterns, especially patterns incorporating commoditized and commercialized attire, entertainment preferences (e.g., music, sports, and movies), lingo, food, and other styles. But the widespread assimilation by no means has eradicated cultural conflict which has, and always will exist as a consequence of social conflict between groups competing for "the rewards and resources of a society or over social values, in which the conflicting parties attempt to neutralize or injure each other" (Newman, 1973, p. 110).

As diverse people come into contact, especially in pluralistic organizations like urban public high schools, they regroup into associations that acknowledge racial and ethnic alliances and other mutual interests. These groups become locked in competition for power, wealth, and position, and they may also engage in fierce disputes over cultural values, norms, and beliefs. They become socially stratified as they jockey for dominance in an effort to retain or improve their positions. They do this in part through the generation of cultures that may affirm ethnic traditions but are just as likely to be highly nuanced versions of the dominant culture. These cultures are the "new" indigenous cultures in the United States with patterns that essentially work to the benefit of the groups who create them. They reflect group interests, and are often perceived by those who attempt to cross between them as being in conflict with, or in opposition to, one another.

The new indigenous cultures in stratified social systems provide the symbolic reference points for the construction and enacting of people's identities. As Appleton (1983) explains, social mobility depends on individuals' ability to belong to *valued* groups or associations that actually provide them with the cultural and social supports they need to realize their full potentials. People must be accepted by, and assimilated into, valued groups where they form and perform empowering identities. Valued groups are those whose members hold powerful positions, enjoy high status, or have access to scarce resources. They also embrace revered religious or secular beliefs. The more groups are esteemed within a society, the more exclusionary they become. Valued groups routinely discriminate against people regarded by members as socially or culturally unacceptable or unable to contribute in any significant way to the promotion of group interests. They limit their membership through enforcement of stringent admissions standards or other types of structural barriers. And they maintain their exclusiveness, and competitive edge, by restricting the transmission of valued cultural systems to those who manage to gain admittance. Valued groups place very real social and cultural constraints on social mobility.

Phelan, Davidson, and Yu (1993, 1998) developed an analytical model couched in the new cultural pluralism they have used to explicate urban high school students' academic achievement. They describe the interrelationships between family, school, and peer worlds, and how the meanings and understandings in these worlds affect students' engagement with learning. They also elucidate students' perceptions of the boundaries and borders between their worlds, and the adaptive strategies they use while moving from one context to another, especially those involving transitions to the world of school. Based on Erickson's (1987) insights, they define *boundaries* as real or perceived lines between worlds, settings, or contexts that are neutral, and where sociocultural components are perceived to be equal. Movement across boundaries occurs with relative ease with little or no social or psychological costs. *Borders*, in marked contrast, are real or perceived lines that are not neutral and separate worlds not perceived as equal. Transitions between worlds with perceived borders can be extremely difficult when the knowledge and skills in one world are more highly valued and esteemed than those in another. While it is possible for students to navigate borders, such transitions may incur significant personal and psychological costs invisible to teachers. Borders become impenetrable barriers when the psychosocial consequences of adaption become too great or valued groups block crossings through pointedly exclusionary social and cultural means. Students in their mediations are also engaging in cultural identity work that is more or less empowering, depending on what happens within or during their crossings between worlds.

The following typology was developed by Phelan et al. (1993) to gage student adaptations with respect to perceived boundaries and borders:

Type I: Congruent Worlds/Smooth Transitions
Type II: Different Worlds/Border Crossings Managed
Type III: Different Worlds/Border Crossings Difficult
Type IV: Different Worlds/Borders Impenetrable

An example of a Type I adaptation drawn from their research is a high school student they pseudonymously named Ryan Moore. Ryan was a European American middle-class student whose worlds were highly congruent. When he left his home in the morning and walked to school with his friends, he experienced extremely smooth social and cultural transitions to the dominant mainstream world of his school. His language and communication styles were the same as those of his teachers, and he fully understood, and was quite adept at deploying strategies necessary for academic success. He knew who had the power; where to go for help; what could or could not be changed; and other rules of the game. His teachers, parents, and friends all regarded Ryan as a "really nice kid, well-liked by everybody" who earned good grades and never got into trouble (Phelan et al., 1993, p. 62). Ryan belonged to valued groups (White middle-class family and peer groups), and was enrolled in exclusive accelerated academic tracks. He rarely interacted with racial and ethnic minority students who, in his opinion, made "our lives miserable here and bring with them the way they hang downtown" (p. 63).

At the other end of the spectrum were students who experienced Type IV adaptations. Sonia Gonzales, Ryan's classmate, is an example of a student who was not able to cross perceived borders. She was a second-generation Mexican American who entered elementary school speaking Spanish. She became English proficient, but lived in a Mexican barrio where she maintained her social and cultural affiliations with her Mexican heritage. She earned mostly Bs and Cs until she entered high school where she failed most of her classes. The borders she encountered in high school became impassable when she moved into a Mexicana peer group with antischool norms. She and other members of the group skipped classes, ignored homework, got into trouble, and became involved in male gang activities. Sonia's difficulties with border crossings were exacerbated by the fact that she had little or no meaningful contact with her teachers, especially White teachers who were, in her estimation, "kind of prejudiced...the way they look at you, the way they talk, you know, when they're talking about something, like when they talk about people who are going to drop out" (Phelan et al., 1993, p. 81). She also experienced little support and occasional hostility from her non-Mexican peers. Sonia felt like an outsider pushed to the sociocultural margins by her teachers and European American middle-class peers. She did not belong to valued groups, and while her Mexican orientation and identity enabled meaningful connections to her home and friends, they disempowered her at school.

Theories in the new cultural pluralism provide insight into students' competing family and peer affiliations; their perceptions of intergroup boundaries and borders; and how transitions to the world of high school are affected by student cultural identity work. But there is more to the story, especially with regards to the historical relationships between dominant White European Americans and various racial and ethnic minority groups and the collective ecological identity work associated with these relations.

Cultural-Ecological Theory

John Ogbu, a distinguished anthropologist who conducted seminal ethnographic research in U.S. high schools, observed in the 1980s how most studies on racial and ethnic minority student academic achievement focused on school failure rather than academic success. While this research sheds light on issues related to particular groups of student underachievers, it did not provide general explanations of achievement patterns because it failed to explain the success of ethnic minority groups who did well in school despite cultural differences, social and workforce discrimination, and other barriers. According to Ogbu (1987), the main factor affecting academic achievement does not lie in the fact that children possess different cultural styles, but rather, "appears to be the nature of the history, subordination, and exploitation of the minorities, *and* the nature of the minorities' own instrumental and expressive responses to their treatment, which enter into the process of their schooling" (p. 317).

Ogbu (1978, 1987, 1991, 1995a, 1995b, 2003; Ogbu & Simons, 1998) developed a general explanation for racial and ethnic minority high school student achievement patterns which he terms the *cultural–ecological theory* (CET). "Ecology," in the theory, is the setting, environment, or world of people, and "cultural" refers to the way people see their world and behave in it. CET has two major parts. One part explains how minorities have been treated and mistreated in terms of educational policies, pedagogical approaches, and returns on their investment in school credentials. Ogbu refers to this part as "the system," which includes the historical practice of denying certain racial and ethnic minority groups access to desirable jobs and positions that require a good education and where education is supposed to pay off. These groups were denied equal economic and educational opportunity through a job ceiling which, as Ogbu explains, discouraged them from pursuing formal educational opportunities.

> By denying the minorities opportunity to gain entry into the labor force and to advance according to their educational qualification and ability, and by denying them adequate rewards for their education in terms of wages, American society discouraged the minorities from investing time and effort into pursuit of education and into maximizing their educational accomplishments. (Ogbu, 1987, p. 318)

Another related societal factor is the historical practice of denying minority groups equal access to good educations. One of the most notable examples is Black Americans who were given inferior educations through formal statutes in the South and informal de facto arrangements in the North.

The second part of the theory focuses on community forces. It explains the impact on minority groups' perceptions of, and cultural responses to, their treatment in the system. Cultural responses are explored as "'collective solutions,' to the collective problems" these groups have confronted for much of their history in the United States (Ogbu & Simons, 1998, p. 158).

In developing this part of the theory, Ogbu constructed a classification system for minority groups enhanced by the concept of the *settler society*. A settler society is one where the dominant group is comprised of immigrants from other societies who came to their new country with the hope of improving their economic, social, and political status. The ancestors of Anglo/European Americans, the dominant group in the United States, were immigrants who transmitted beliefs in self-improvement through hard work and individual responsibility, and promoted assimilation into a common culture.

Another feature of settler societies is that they usually have at least two types of minorities: those who have come for the same reasons as the dominant group, and those who were forced into the society against their will. The statuses of these groups are affected by power relations. Groups in the United States become a "minority" not because of their numbers but, rather, because they occupy a subordinate power position in relation to the dominant group.

Ogbu (1987; Ogbu & Simons, 1998) breaks down minority group classifications even further into *autonomous, voluntary* (immigrant), and *involuntary* (nonimmigrant) statuses. Autonomous minorities, such as Jews, Amish, and Mormons, are relatively small in number. While they may have suffered discrimination, they were not totally dominated or oppressed, and their school achievement is no different from that of the dominant group. Voluntary minorities, such as immigrants from Africa, Cuba, China, India, Japan, Korea, Central and South America, the Caribbean (Jamaica, Trinidad, the Dominican Republic), and Mexico, moved to the United States more or less willingly. They voluntarily chose to immigrate to improve their lot in life, and do not interpret their presence as somehow forced upon them by the government or dominant group. They usually experience some academic difficulties in school when they first arrive because of discriminatory educational policies and practices and language and cultural differences. But they do not experience long-lasting adjustment problems because they are convinced discrimination is temporary, and that cultural and language accommodations will improve their chances for socioeconomic success.

Involuntary nonimmigrant minorities were conquered, colonized, or enslaved and include African Americans who were brought to the United States as slaves; American Indians and Alaskan natives, and Mexican Americans in the Southwest, who were conquered; native Hawaiians who were colonized; and Puerto Ricans who consider themselves a colonized people. These groups became a permanent part of U.S. society against their will and interpret their presence as forced on them by White people. They are less economically successful than voluntary minorities and usually experience much greater, more persistent language and cultural difficulties. They also do less well in school.

Involuntary minorities have been historically "castelike" in their relations with the dominant group. They were relegated to menial positions and denied true assimilation into mainstream society. They developed a strong sense of peoplehood and collective identity in response to their subjugation. And they adopted cultural traits that were somewhat different from, and expressed in opposition to, those condoned by dominant White groups.

Cultural differences and cultural identity in relation to dominant groups are key to understanding racial and ethnic minority student academic achievement patterns (Ogbu, 1987). Voluntary immigrant groups are characterized by primary cultural differences in relation to dominant groups, and involuntary or castelike minorities are characterized by secondary cultural differences. Primary cultural differences are differences that exist *before* two populations come into contact. They may pose difficulties for voluntary immigrant students when they first enter school, but they are often overcome through the determination of students who strive to fit in (accommodate) in order to succeed. These students believe that such accommodations will lead to better lives. Rather than feeling they are losing their native cultures and identities, they believe they are adding to their cultural and identity repertoires. Accommodation is an additive rather than a subtractive process for them.

Secondary cultural differences, common among involuntary minorities, arise *after* group participation in institutions such as schools, which are controlled by another group. They are formed in response to contact situations where one group is being dominated by another. Secondary cultural differences are usually expressed as differences in style, such as styles of communication, dress, interaction, and learning. Style is related to *cultural inversion,* which is the tendency for members of involuntary minorities to regard certain forms of behaviors, events, symbols, and meanings as inappropriate for them because they are characteristic of White Americans. What come to be regarded as appropriate styles for them are defined *in opposition to* the practices and preferences of White Americans. They are, in essence, expressions of resistance.

After their subordination, involuntary minorities have also developed a sense of social identity in opposition to the social identity of the dominant group. They have done this in response to the ways the dominant group treated them, particularly with regard to how they were deliberately excluded from true assimilation into the dominant culture, or the reverse, were forced to assimilate. Their social identity is collective in the sense that it is shared by most members of the group and passed on from generation to generation.

Involuntary minorities also have a dual frame of reference. The first frame is their socioeconomic status in the United States. The second is the socioeconomic status of middle-class White Americans. This comparison is a negative one because involuntary minorities see their status, as well as their schools, as inferior to those of Whites. They do not believe that the United States is a land of opportunity where anyone who works hard and has a good education will obtain upward mobility. They believe that racism and discrimination is a permanent feature of U.S. society.

The instrumental response that involuntary minorities have to their inferior status and schools is an ambivalent folk theory of making it, which, on the one hand, endorses the ethic of hard work and the value of education while, on the other hand, reinforces the belief that hard work and school achievement will not overcome institutionalized racism and discrimination. Involuntary minority children are deeply affected by this ambivalence. Rather than admire and emulate successful minority professionals as role models, they often view them with suspicion. They suspect that these professionals adopted White ways, such as speaking Standard English, and otherwise gave in to the White oppressor and abandoned their minority group identity in the process. Adopting White ways in order to succeed is experienced as a subtractive process that threatens collective identity. School cultural requirements, especially expectations to speak and write Standard English, are the biggest signifier of someone who is "acting White" and has sold out to Whites.

Signithia Fordham (1988, 1996, 2008; Fordham & Ogbu, 1986) applied Ogbu's theory in her ethnographic research in an urban high school she pseudonymously named Capital High. She found that oppositional identity work had a profound impact on Black students' perceptions and interpretation of schooling. They viewed schooling as learning White American cultural frames of reference with negative consequences for the integrity of their Black cultural identities and cultural commitments. Learning school curriculum and conforming to standard classroom practices were equated with "acting White" and forsaking acting Black. Schooling was regarded as a subtractive process causing many Black students to hide or reject "White" academic identities, and downplay or resist academic achievement. They not only did this in the classroom, but also socially in their peer groups and psychologically as individuals. Black peer groups discouraged members from putting forth the time and effort required to do well in school. Psychologically, Black students were not inclined to strive academically out of fear of negative peer reprisals, and also to avoid affective dissonance.

Black students who wanted to achieve in school had to deal with the "burden" of acting White. To act White, Fordham (2008) explains, "was most clearly manifested in having power over other Black people, a burden reeking with identity conflict" (p. 232):

> Required to fulfill White cultural norms, [Black students] still might be excluded from the economic and social rewards of academic success. Their "stolen" White identity (aka attempted identity theft) was double sided: Black high achievers were compelled both to be and not to be socially White, to respect and retain their citizenship in the Black community while struggling for recognition in the dominant White society. Many sought to convey the impression that they were not concerned with academic excellence—if only as a cover for their real ambition. (Fordham, 2008, p. 232)

Black students at Capital High who wanted to achieve academically were afraid of being labeled "brainiacs" (tantamount to being labeled "White") which some described as the "kiss of death." They covered up their academic efforts, and adopted various cultural boundary-maintaining devices. Shelvy, one of the Black students profiled in Fordham's study, purposely lowered her effort in school. When she was called upon by teachers to answer questions, she responded quickly and correctly but, in her words, "put brakes" on high levels of academic performance to deflect negative peer reprisals. Martin was a high achiever who adopted social devices that cloaked his accomplishments to minimize hostilities directed at him as an academically successful student. One such cloaking device was "lunching" where he acted "crazy" so he would not be called a brainiac, or have his manhood called into question.

> Okay. Lunching is like when you be acting crazy, you know, having fun with women, you know. Okay, you still be going to class, but you—like me, okay, they call me crazy, 'cause I'll be having fun. (Fordham & Ogbu, 1986, p. 194)

The burden of acting White was shouldered differently by girls and boys. Resistance among Black girls was rampant, but it was riddled with contradictions. Black girls are raised to reject the emulation of White female bodies and exemplify what the Black community deems appropriate for strong Black women. But they are also encouraged to conform to dominant group expectations for successful girls. "[Black] parents seek to rear their daughters to be both survivors and 'ladies,'" Fordham (1996) explains, "the latter embodying those characteristics traditionally affiliated with upper-class White womanhood" (p. 104). These mixed messages get tangled up in Black girls' identity work as a matter of survival as well as a desire to be able "to do anything anyone else can do" including acting White.

The contradictions that Black boys confront are deeply implicated in a society that "favors maleness but debases Blackness" (Fordham, 1996, p. 165). Blacks boys feel compelled to resist their subservient place in the race hierarchy while, at the same time, conform to dominant norms and values associated with White patriarchal manhood. They resolve the tension by adopting conspicuous, somewhat aggressive styles that stigmatize them in ways that ensure their "confinement to secondary domination."

Ogbu's cultural–ecological theory and the acting White hypothesis developed in Fordham's work continue to resonate in anthropological scholarship. While their ideas are groundbreaking and certainly provocative, they have been challenged as being too deterministic, and treating high achievement among involuntary minority students, especially Black students, as generally exceptional (Horvat & O'Connor, 2006; O'Connor, 1997). The significant variation in academic achievement within and between student peer groups is underplayed, and not enough emphasis is placed on the fact that school contexts, the staging areas for student cultural work vary, often considerably. Context matters enormously with regards to how cultural differences and cultural and academic identities are ultimately negotiated and expressed by high school students (Andrews, 2009; Hemmings, 1996, 1998).

The powerful effects of social class are also downplayed. Wealth on some educational measures virtually eradicates statistically significant differences between Black and White student achievement patterns (Conley, 1999). And while Fordham does attend to differences between boys and girls, her analysis does not go far enough to expose the highly nuanced constructions of masculinity and femininity in racial and ethnic minority students' identity work. Nor does it reveal the complex and politically charged ways in which "Whiteness" and "Blackness" intersect with ethnicity in urban high schools that serve several racial and ethnic minority groups. Another limitation of this theory is its somewhat restricted view of the experiences of immigrant youth, especially the growing number of children of immigrants of color in American cities.

Segmented Assimilation

Immigrants have always been a part of the story of urban public high schools. Prior to 1965 when legislation changed national origin quotas for immigration, a significant number of immigrants came from the United Kingdom, Ireland, and Western and Eastern Europe. They were mostly White and embraced customs with historical linkages to those associated with 17th and 18th century Anglo/European colonizers. The 1965 Hart-Celler immigration reforms put an end to those quotas in U.S. immigration policy and opened the door to immigrants from other countries. These post-Hart-Celler immigrants and their children constitute a majority of the population in many large cities, including New York, Miami, and Los Angeles (Kasinitz et al., 2008). In New York City, for example, 2005 Current Population Survey data indicate that 35% of the population is foreign born and their native born children constitute around 17% of the population. Among young adults ages 18 to 32, more than a fifth were born to immigrant parents and another fifth arrived by age 12. Immigrant people, and especially their children, are reshaping American urban life and achieving mobility in remarkable and culturally creative ways.

People of color constitute a large proportion of both the most recent wave of immigrants and earlier waves following World War II. Among them are West Indians from Jamaica, Belize, the Virgin Islands, and other parts of the Caribbean. In the 1940s, immigrants from India migrated to the United States after India gained independence from England in 1947. They included Sikhs who had once enjoyed a privileged relationship with British colonial rulers but, as immigrants to the United States and United Kingdom, found themselves being grouped together with other collectively "Black" people (Hall, 2002). Immigrants from Africa, the Dominican Republic, and other countries are also relegated to such groupings.

Regardless of their national origin, immigrants are typically assigned to "proximal host" categories such as "Black" African American, American Jew, and Hispanic (Mittelberg & Waters, 1992). Russian Jews, for example, are regarded as American Jews. Black African Americans are the proximal host for West Indians and Sikhs because White Americans generally do not differentiate among people with black skin. Despite being lumped together into entrenched racial categories, many of the children of immigrants of color are achieving a higher level of education than African Americans and other native-born people of color (Logan & Deane, 2003). Scholars often turn to Ogbu's cultural–ecological theory to explain the disparity. But CET does not delve deeply enough into the variety of paths taken by immigrants, nor does it adequately address the effects of race, ethnicity, social class, and other social locations on social mobility. What is missing, according to Butterfield (2006), is an analysis of how children of immigrants, particularly children of Black immigrants, complicate some of the fundamental premises of the CET model regarding achievement and perceptions of socioeconomic opportunity. In an interview study she conducted of the children of West Indian immigrants, including low-income, working-class, and middle-class respondents, Butterfield found that people of West Indian descent who were raised primarily in the United States did not necessarily consider themselves guests in a foreign land nor did they consider social barriers, particularly those related to race, as temporary. And yet they still achieved at higher levels than their African American counterparts.

Another theoretical approach that better explains such disparities is the *segmented assimilation* model developed by Portes and Zhou (1993). The model posits that immigrant students of color take different paths to acculturation. They may incorporate themselves into Anglo/European mainstream (White) middle-class culture; assimilate into underclass racial or ethnic minority groups; or utilize the cultural capital of their own immigrant communities to navigate opportunities. Assimilation into African American, Latino, or other historically marginalized groups is regarded by many immigrants of color as a path leading to downward mobility. Many of them intentionally disassociate themselves from African and Latino Americans and do not regard success in school as "acting White" or somehow compromising who they are or their group affiliations.

The segmented assimilation model also posits that the varying modes of incorporation of the first generation endows the second generation with differing amounts of cultural and social capital in the forms of ethnic jobs, networks, values, and exposure to different opportunities. The West Indians in Butterfield's (2006) study faced racial barriers and believed that these barriers would always be there. But they surmounted them by employing adaption strategies that included family involvement in education, high standards for achievement set by parents and peer groups, and the use of ethnic social networks.

Kasinitz et al. (2008) conducted a much more expansive multiethnic and racial study of second generation urban immigrants. They interviewed 3,415 young adult (aged 18 to 32) second and 1.5 generation (individuals born abroad who arrived to the United States by age 12) Dominican, Colombian, Ecuadorian, Peruvian, West Indian, Chinese, Russian Jews, and native White and Black comparison groups in and around New York City. Six ethnographers also collected data in high schools, university campuses, workplaces, churches, and other places. Except for the Dominican men of color in their sample, there was little evidence of second-generation educational and socioeconomic decline. Participants were doing at least somewhat better than natives of the same race, even after adjusting for social class and other advantages in family background. They were not achieving success by clinging to the networks and enclaves of their immigrant communities. Nor were they simply joining the mainstream. What many of them did was take advantage of their "in between-ness" by negotiating different combinations of immigrant and native advantages and choosing the best combinations for themselves. They yielded distinct second-generation advantages by selecting the best traits from their immigrant parents and their peers with native-born parents.

> These traits include a position in society—living in certain neighborhoods, having certain jobs, being treated by the larger society in a certain way—and participating in a shared culture—holding certain norms and having specific repertoires about how to be in the world. None of these are uniform across all individuals in a group—individuals differ in how much they identify with ethnicity, with how varied their social networks are, and in how much they internalize and act on norms and values they inherit from their parents and extended family. (Kasinitz et al., 2008, p. 67)

Being "in between" has enabled many children of immigrants to engage in forms of cultural innovation that New Yorkers and inhabitants of other cities have received well. They not only belong to ethnic groups, but also to social classes, genders, social groups, and neighborhoods. Like all contemporary Americans, they work with and through a multiplicity of interacting social roles and identities.

Kasinitz et al. (2008) also observed how many children of immigrants of color have benefitted from civil rights era policies and institutions initially designed to help African Americans and Puerto Ricans. While originally intended to address the age-old racial cleavages in American society, such policies have proved advantageous in easing the incorporation of immigrants of color and their children. Being racialized as a member of a minority group has positive effects that can offset some of the negative effects stressed by segmented assimilation theory. The children and other descendents of immigrants who are living in urban areas are remaking mainstream culture with creative energy by drawing from several cultural sources. It is "cool" to be multiculturally adaptive and to hang out with different kinds of people. The children of urban immigrants are at the vanguard of cultural hybridity and finding rewards in their cultural innovations.

Although the children of immigrants of color appear to have some advantages, many of them are attending urban public high schools characterized by a politics of racialized identity work that can have a profound and decisively negative impact on their achievement.

Racial Formation Theory

The cultural identity work of involuntary minorities, as Ogbu and Fordham point out, is fueled by collective struggles; binds communities together into bounded collectives; and is a powerful impetus for collective responses to societal injustices and discriminatory institutional practices. Researchers often construe identity work as a bipolar (Black pole vs. White pole) process when it involves African Americans and Anglo/European Americans, with people from other ethnic groups treated separately and regarded as somewhat raceless. But race intersects with ethnicity, and also with social class and gender, in ways that profoundly shape identity work across racial and ethnic groups in the United States. This fact is the basis for *racial formation theory* which recognizes how students in multiracial and multiethnic high schools assert and defend themselves through racialized identity work characterized by racial identifications and performances that are forged through relational politics; permeated with social class influences; imbued with ethnic cultural commitments; linked to gendered notions of masculinity and femininity; and structured by the contours of institutional forces (Omi & Winant, 1994; Staiger, 2006).

Annegret Daniela Staiger (2006) rendered racial formation theory into a framework for analyzing the identity work of urban high school students. American cities, she observes, have experienced significant changes in their population demographics and are increasingly multiracial and multiethnic. Urban high schools now more than ever are serving students from numerous indigenous, immigrant, refugee, and transient groups where members' racial, ethnic, social class, and gender locations are quite entangled and not so clear cut. Anglo/European Americans are becoming a minority in many urban areas, and yet urban public schools continue to affirm the mainstream cultural commitments of dominant middle-class Anglo/European American groups. What race means to students in these schools has changed, and these meanings are infused into identity work through "racial projects" where students actively shape and reshape racial orders (Staiger, 2006, p. 11). Rather than involving two opposing racial groups, Blacks and Whites, these projects involve many groups who forge their identities during the course of their ongoing relations with one another. Identity work is thus relational, and it is also racialized as it plays out, and falls along, a discursive continuum of "Whiteness" and "Blackness." Students in multiracial and multiethnic urban high schools are constantly managing their relationships with other racialized groups both in individual and collective terms.

Students are political in their identity work. They deploy strategic identity markers in the establishment of social boundaries and hierarchies, creation of allegiances, solidification of alliances, and assertions of dominance. Urban youths, Staiger (2006) explains, are "political actors with an analytical acumen for assessing and forming power structures, recognizing and establishing hierarchies, and ascribing political motives to larger collective identities" (p. 5). Race in their political maneuverings is a shorthand way for them to identify motives, group interests, and enemies. It can be used to stigmatize rival groups, or as a valuable form of social capital.

Racial formation theory also recognizes how cultural identity work intersects with social class, gender, and ethnic community allegiances. Students have different social and educational advantages and disadvantages depending on their social class backgrounds. Middle-class students have much more economic, social, cultural, and symbolic capital than working- and lower-class students, and they expend this capital to maintain their positions and identities as members of valued groups. Students also produce expressions of masculinity and femininity in their identity performances, and display loyalties to their natal ethnic communities through language and dress codes, religion and religious customs, and other cultural demonstrations. All of this complex identity work is done within public high schools structured by powerful institutional forces that keep racialized groups apart. Among these structures is tracking where racialized student groups are typically segregated into hierarchically differentiated classes where labels like "gifted" and "at risk" become institutionalized and function as code words for race, and discourses that effectively substantiate differences in the academic abilities and achievement of different racialized groups.

Staiger (2006) applied racial formation theory in an ethnographic study of Roosevelt High, a multiracial high school in California heralded for its academic excellence and racial harmony. The school served African American, Cambodian, Latino, Samoan, and White Anglo/European American students. There was a hierarchical political configuration among students with working-class and low-income African Americans at the top with their conspicuously flashy clothing styles, colorful vernacular, and intense policing of racial boundaries. Cambodians, who were in conflict with Latinos, were the "Blacks of the Asians." Descended from refugees of the Vietnam War, they forged alliances with dominant African Americans that were more culturally symbolic than socially authentic. Latinos, some of whom spoke Spanish, lived in residentially segregated working- and middle-class communities established in the 1930s. They were the most vulnerable group because of a movement in the state to pass a proposition to drastically limit social services to undocumented immigrants. They gravitated toward White Anglo/European American students who, ironically, were most representative of the groups supporting the proposition. Samoans were immigrants who wore traditional garb and carried themselves with an assured dignity that garnered much respect and high status.

Students were tracked into GROW, a magnet program for gifted students, and other academies including business and technology (BusTech) widely considered to be the lowest track. A discourse of protection shielded the mostly middle-class White students in the GROW program from the mostly low-income Black and Black-racialized students in the BusTech program. GROW students, including students of color, were Whitened against a discursive backdrop of non-Whiteness and nongiftedness. BusTech students were Blackened and absorbed in a program culture imbued with the discourse of acting White (à la Ogbu and Fordham) with its collective ethos of opposition, including opposition to schooling. They flaunted and played with racist stereotypes through signifying and other racially affirmative means.

Males in their identity work performed masculinities through racial matrices. African American, Cambodian, and Latino males utilized racialized discourses in efforts to establish their dominance. Their performances revolved around men's relationships with women, other men, and within and between groups. Some were disturbingly violent even deadly, such as those among Cambodian males who gauged their manhood by fighting, killing people, and otherwise "putting in work" in local gangs. Masculinities constructed around men's relationships with women were blatantly manipulative. African American young men revered "pimps" who garnered money and other resources from women and "players" who had multiple sex partners. Women, for their part, would play along with men through sexualized expressions of femininity, or would resist male dominance or sexual harassment through their own appropriations of racialized discourses of masculinity. They would fight back, sometimes physically, and also fight with other young women who were threatening their relations with males or their social position.

Tensions between groups sometimes came to a violent head like those ignited by a fight between African American girls and a group of Latinas that led to a race riot in the schoolyard. Samoans stepped in as mediators, quelled the riot, and thereafter become known as the peacemakers. But they were not always present or able to mediate conflicts between student groups with entrenched hostilities toward one another.

Teachers and administrators at Roosevelt High were present and certainly involved in identity work and other cultural processes. But Staiger did not delve into the critical roles they played nor, for that matter, do most other studies focusing on urban high school students. Teachers, administrators, and other school actors are, as critical matter of fact, very much involved in school cultural productions.

CONCEPT BOX 3.5

Cultural Theories: Racial and Ethnic Minority Student Achievement

Cultural Deficit	Racial and ethnic minority students are deficient in language skills, social development, intellectual ability, and other areas needed to succeed in school.
Home— School Cultural Discontinuity	Cultural patterns of learning, communication, and literary and writing styles racial and ethnic minority students learn at home are different from those that teachers expect at school.
	Home–school cultural discontinuities provoke misunderstandings and problematic classroom interactions that can escalate over time and ultimately lead to academic trouble and failure.
	Racial and ethnic minority students are essentially caught between two worlds. They confront a painful choice between staying true to their natal communities or assimilation into the world of their schools.
New Cultural Pluralism	Emphasis on critical relationship between cultural diversity and social stratification in an era of increasing urbanization. Ethnic groups are no longer bounded communities with stable ways of life. Community cultural systems constantly change through intergroup appropriations, resistances, and accommodations.
	Social conflict is a catalyst for cultural conflict. Groups become socially stratified as they jockey for dominance. They generate cultures that may affirm ethnic traditions and also include elements of the dominant culture. Cultures reflect group interests and are in conflict with one another.
	Group cultures in stratified social systems provide the symbolic reference points for identities. Social mobility depends on people's ability to belong to valued groups where they develop empowering identities and are provided with sociocultural supports. Valued groups are those whose members hold powerful positions, enjoy high status, and have access to scarce resources.

Boundaries are perceived as neutral lines and sociocultural components as equal across worlds. Movement across boundaries occurs with relative ease. Borders are perceived as lines between separate and unequal worlds. Transitions are difficult when the knowledge and skills in one world are more highly valued than those in another. Borders become impenetrable barriers when the psychosocial consequences of adaption become too great, or when valued groups block crossings through exclusionary means.

Types of student adaptations with respect to perceived boundaries and borders:

Type I: Congruent Worlds/Smooth Transitions
Type II: Different Worlds/Border Crossings Managed
Type III: Different Worlds/Border Crossings Difficult
Type IV: Different Worlds/Borders Impenetrable

Cultural– Ecological Theory (CET)

Certain racial and ethnic minority groups were mistreated in terms of educational policies, pedagogical approaches, and returns on their investment in school credentials. The "system" denied them equal economic opportunity through job ceilings which discouraged them from pursuing formal educational opportunities.

Community forces have had a profound impact on minority groups' perceptions of, and cultural responses to, their mistreatment in the system. Cultural responses are collective solutions to collective problems.

Minority groups have different statuses. Autonomous minorities were not totally dominated, and their school achievement is no different from that of the dominant group. Voluntary (immigrant) minorities came to the United States to improve their lives, and do not interpret their presence as somehow forced upon them. Their school adjustment problems are temporary. Involuntary (nonimmigrant) minorities were conquered, colonized, or enslaved. They interpret their presence in U.S. society as forced on them by White people and were historically "castelike" in their relations with the dominant group. They have long-term adjustment problems in schools.

CONCEPT BOX 3.5 *Continued*

Voluntary immigrant groups are characterized by primary cultural differences in relation to dominant groups. Involuntary minorities are characterized by secondary cultural differences. Primary cultural differences exist before two populations come into contact and are overcome through accommodations regarded as additive. Secondary cultural differences arise after group participation in ongoing contact situations where one group is dominating another. They are often expressed through cultural inversions of style where certain forms of behaviors, events, symbols, and meanings are deemed inappropriate because of their associations with White people.

The adoption of White ways is regarded as a subtractive process threatening collective social identity. Accommodations to school cultural requirements are signifiers of someone who is "acting White" and selling out. Involuntary minority students may express their cultural identities in symbolic opposition to Whites.

Segmented Assimilation   Immigrant students take different paths to acculturation. They may incorporate themselves into Anglo/European mainstream (White) middle-class culture; assimilate into underclass racial or ethnic minority groups; or utilize the cultural capital of their own immigrant communities. Assimilation into African American, Latino, or other historically marginalized groups is a path leading to downward mobility.

The varying modes of incorporation of the first generation endows the second generation with differing amounts of cultural and social capital in the forms of ethnic jobs, networks, values, and exposure to different opportunities. This affects the allegiances of the second generation.

Racial   Students in multiracial and multiethnic urban schools
Formation   assert and defend themselves through racialized identity work characterized by racial identifications and performances that are forged through relational politics; permeated with social class influences; imbued with ethnic cultural commitments; linked to gendered notions of masculinity and femininity; and structured by the contours of institutional forces.

The meaning of race is infused into identity work through "racial projects" where students actively shape and reshape racial orders. Identity work plays out, and falls along, a discursive continuum of "Whiteness" and "Blackness."

Students are political in their identity work. They deploy strategic identity markers in the establishment of social boundaries and hierarchies, creation of allegiances, solidification of alliances, and assertions of dominance. Race is a shorthand way for them to identify motives, group interests, and enemies. It can be used to stigmatize rival groups, or as a valuable form of social capital.

Identity work intersects with social class, gender, and ethnicity. Students have different social and educational advantages and disadvantages depending on their social class backgrounds. They produce expressions of masculinity and femininity through racial matrices, and display affiliations with their natal ethnic communities through language and dress codes, religion and religious customs, and other cultural demonstrations.

Identity work within public high schools is structured by powerful institutional forces that keep racialized groups apart. Among these structures is tracking where racialized student groups are typically segregated into hierarchically differentiated programs and classes. Students in upper-track classes are Whitened against a discursive backdrop of non-Whiteness and nongiftedness. Lower-track students are Blackened and absorbed into program cultures imbued with the discourse of acting white with its collective ethos of opposition including opposition to schooling. They flaunt and play with racist stereotypes through signifying and other racially affirmative means.

Cultural Challenges of Religious Minorities

Cultural theories that focus on the academic achievement of racial and ethnic minority high school students generally do not address the powerful influences of organized religion, religious identity, and allegiances to religious communities. They underconceptualize or ignore the cultural challenges faced by religious minorities, and how public schools accommodate, mediate, or exacerbate religious differences.

Survey data collected by the Pew Research Center (2010) confirm the well-known fact that Protestants are the largest proportion of U.S. residents who claim some affiliation with organized religion. Twenty-six percent are associated with an array of Evangelical Protestant denominations and 18% are mainline Protestants (e.g. Baptist, Methodist, Lutheran, Presbyterian, Congregationalist, and Anglican/Episcopal). They coexist with Roman Catholics, members of historically Black churches (HBC), Mormons, Orthodox Greeks and Russians, Jews, Muslims and other religious minorities. Twenty-three percent of people in the United States identify themselves as Roman Catholic; 7% percent belong to HBCs; 1.7% are Mormon; and .6% are Greek and Russian Orthodox. Other statistically small but conspicuous religious minorities include Jews (1.7%) and Muslims (.6%).

Public schooling had a Protestant bent until a series of Supreme Court rulings banned prayer, Bible scripture readings, explicit religious instruction, and other Protestant-based practices in public schools (McCarthy, 1985). There has always been an historical discrepancy between American principles of religious freedom and the practice of religion in public institutions. Constitutional or not, religion, especially Christianity, is influential in many public institutions, including public high schools.

I learned in a study I conducted of adolescent coming of age processes in U.S. high schools that religion looms large in the lives of students (Hemmings, 2004). So large, in fact, that I was compelled to delve into students' religious identities and navigations of religious beliefs, values, and practices. Participants in the research were thoughtful and very serious about religion as they sorted out their own beliefs about God and the supernatural; held fast to or broke away from organized religions; and wrestled with morality. They exercised their right to seek freedom of and from religion.

I also found that Protestant and Roman Catholic students' religious quests and questionings generally did not conflict with the academic curriculum, extracurricular activities, holiday observances, and other public school conventions. They were able to reconcile religious practices with school practices. All religions have disciplinary practices intended to hold adherents to doctrinally sanctioned patterns of beliefs, values, and norms. Practices include the daily discipline of prayer, meditation or scripture reading, and ceremonial rites and rituals that mark significant religious events and life passages. There are also practices that discipline the body through dress codes as well as norms that place constraints on sexual activity, diet, the use of intoxicants, and so forth. Marriage, work, and other areas of life also are regulated by practices supported by the moral authority of sacred scriptures and religious leaders.

Expressing religious practices is the most obvious outward sign that an individual has made a commitment to, or is being effectively disciplined by, a religion. While overtly religious Christian practices (e.g., prayer and scripture reading) are not allowed in public schools, other practices in sync with Christian customs permeate schools' cultural ethos.

Non-Christian students, especially those who have immigrated with their parents to American cities, are much more likely to experience conflict between religious practices and school practices. Some, like Russian Jews, are assimilating into secular mainstream Anglo/European (Christian) culture and achieving in school while simultaneously dealing with pressures to be more religious. A huge wave of Jewish immigrants arrived between 1882 and 1924 that eventually coalesced into one of the most powerful ethnic communities in urban areas. The Jewish community established an extensive network of social and religious institutions that by the 1980s began to run out of traditional clients, which caused them to focus more attention on new arrivals (Kasinitz et al., 2008). Many young Jews and second-generation Russian Jews are under pressure to be more observant in ways that have complicated their cultural adaptations. But this has not, by and large, affected their ability or willingness to fit into public school cultural milieu. They are among the groups with high graduation and college attendance rates.

The experiences of Muslims are qualitatively different, particularly among those determined to preserve their Islamic traditions. Muslims, especially Arabs from the Middle East, are becoming a more pronounced presence in American cities. They have been immigrating to the United States for more than a century. Most in the past assimilated into mainstream culture, especially Arab immigrants who were formally educated and held professional positions (Naff, 1985, 1994). Recent immigrants, especially Yemenis and Iraqis who arrived in the last 30 years are typically from the peasant classes in their countries. Unlike many of their Arab predecessors, they resist assimilation and adhere more strictly to conservative Islamic religious practices.

Sarroub (2005) conducted an intriguing study of conservative Yemeni *hijabat* girls who attended a high school in Dearborn, Michigan pseudonymously named Cobb High. The girls were identified as *hijabat* because they donned the *hijab,* veils worn by women in their communities. They were the children of Yemeni parents who moved to the Detroit area because of blue-collar jobs in the shipping and auto industries. Many parents did not have formal schooling and were illiterate or semiliterate in Arabic and English. They maintained strong ties with their homeland. They purchased land in Yemen with the intent of going back; visited Yemen for long periods of time; and sent their children there to marry. Their children straddled two worlds: the predominantly Christian world of U.S. society and the family and neighborhood world of Yemeni culture and Islamic religious traditions firmly rooted in the Qur'an.

The immigration of Yemeni, Iraqi, and other conservative Muslims in the United States has coincided with an explosive growth of worldwide Islamic conservatism in the wake of American proprietary interests in Arab oil production and wars in Iraq and Afghanistan. Friction between majority Christian and minority Muslim religious groups has swelled and is posing difficult challenges for Muslim students in urban public high schools.

The challenge at Cobb High was met head-on. Teachers and administrators made an intentional effort to accommodate the Muslim traditions of Yemeni students. They implemented formal and informal curricular strategies that included resource material about Muslims, a bilingual program, Friday afternoon leave for Islamic religious instruction, consultation and sensitivity to religious differences, adaptation of the physical education curriculum, and sensitivity to swimwear deemed appropriate for *hijabat* girls. They also adopted informal measures including dietary accommodations, the establishment of a diversity club, the use of dual language signs within the school, and the recognition of Muslim holidays.

Despite these well-intended accommodations, teachers often found themselves caught in the middle as enforcers of unenforceable measures to uphold Muslim religious traditions and at the same time acting as agents of non-Muslim American culture. Muslim students complained about teachers who were perceived as prejudiced and a group of Yemeni *hijabat* at one point presented a list of grievances to administrators. There were fights between Arab and non-Arab students and teachers noted a pervasive lack of academic engagement among Yemeni boys who were prone to cheat on assignments.

Hijabat girls were especially challenged by the conflicting pressures they encountered in their worlds. They were also the most creative in their negotiations of cultural divides. Most of them claimed primary allegiance to their Yemeni families, Arabs in general, and Islam in particular. They avoided contact with male peers partly because they were under constant surveillance by newly arrived "boater" Yemeni boys. They understood that if their reputations were tarnished, they would be taken out of school and sent to Yemen where they would be married or cursed. They also excelled in their studies to make sure that they would not be sent to Yemen.

Despite the enormous pressure on them to comply with conservative Yemeni Muslim traditions, many of the *hijabat* girls managed to navigate their own life courses. One who was especially adamant that Cobb High accommodate Yemeni traditions was able to choose her own husband despite pressure at home to accept an arranged marriage. Other girls entered community colleges after high school graduation or found work at a local community center. Another girl was placed under FBI protection after she was kidnapped by her parents who wanted to send her to Yemen because she refused to marry her cousin, wear the *hijab*, and settle in the neighborhood.

The challenges for conservative Muslims have been intensified in a country that is increasingly anti-Muslim. Many Christian Americans in the wake of the September 11, 2011 airplane attacks on U.S. buildings view Muslims, including those who have been residing in the country for generations, as suspect, anti-American, or dangerous radicals. This does not bode well for Muslim youths attending public high schools.

Cultural Production in Urban Schools

School actors, regardless of their racial, ethnic, and religious backgrounds are all engaged in school cultural processes. Teachers are especially caught up in cultural negotiations that put them on the frontlines of cultural conflict sometimes to the point of outright warfare (Hemmings, 2002, 2003). Battles are fought where teachers in defense of the dominant cultural regime of schooling pit themselves against racial and ethnic minority students who feel they are being misunderstood, disrespected, or neglected. Clashes can be fierce and psychologically damaging, with casualties on both sides.

Partly in recognition of the need to focus more attention on conflict and how to resolve it, some educational anthropologists are reenvisioning school cultural processes as cultural productions involving all actors in local school settings—students, teachers, administrators, parents, and community members—supported by research and theory intentionally geared toward the generation of more socially and culturally constructive pedagogical practices. Rather than focus on academic achievement gaps and study such gaps largely in terms of student adaptations to school culture, schooling is conceived as cultural productions where symbolic forms are "created within the structural constraints of sites such as schools, [and] subjectivities form and agency develops" (Levinson & Holland, 1996, p. 14). Patterns of schooling and identity work are historical and situational; constructed and maintained interactively; challenged through political processes; and thus culturally produced (Carspeken, 2002; Levinson & Holland, 1996).

School actors are recognized as producers of fluid cultures rather than adaptors to static cultures. They do not simply accommodate or resist mainstream school culture but rather actively participate in the production of the patterns of everyday life in classrooms, corridors, and administrative offices. These patterns are constructive if they pull school actors together in the production of meaningful and empowering educational opportunities. They are destructive if they tear people apart, incite seemingly intractable conflict, or cause students to drop out of school and good teachers to quit. School actors in any case manufacture their own cultural worlds and do so under powerful organizational and external constraints. They produce symbolic forms within discriminatory structures, such as tracking, and against the controlling cultural pressures and policies of dominant groups.

Educational anthropologists are promoting, and at some school sites, actually implementing strategies for constructive cultural productions. One strategy, long proposed by George Spindler (1999, 2002; Spindler & Spindler, 1993), is based on the observation that many teachers have false assumptions or illusions about racial and ethnic minority students because they do not fully comprehend students' sociocultural realities. "The basic idea," he writes, "is that whole school systems ... may be centered on illusions about the nature of the situation they are dealing with, and responsible people will make decisions on the basis of them" (Spindler, 2002, p. 18). These illusions are deeply rooted in latent belief systems, and penetrating them is a critical step in constructive cultural production.

The penetration of illusions commences with ethnographic research, anthropologists' signature method of inquiry, as the most effective way to uncover the sociocultural realities of students. Ethnography can foster healing, or what Spindler (1999; Spindler & Spindler, 1993) terms "cultural therapy," as researchers dig through layers of false assumptions in an effort to expose, and ultimately recognize, students' real experiences and aspirations for themselves.

Ethnography can also be an effectual means for the facilitation of constructive identity work leading to self-clarification or restorative self-recognition (Trueba, 1993). I conducted such ethnographic research with a group of urban high school students who had engaged in oppositional identity work that caused severe breakages with schools, families, peers, churches, and other worlds (Hemmings, 2000b). The group included Black and White youths, gays and lesbians, a brain-injured boy, teenage mothers and expectant mothers, high achievers, and low achievers. Lona Young, a working-class Black girl, was a central figure in the group who forged cultural linkages that enabled group members to clarify and affirm their "true" selves, and express their identities in ethical relation to others. Lona's links engendered a restorative form of cultural therapy, and a politics of reconciliation, that empowered students to resituate their selves within, and in some cases, transform their worlds.

Ethnography aimed at positive cultural productions need not be carried out exclusively by adult researchers. It can be much more effective if it involves students. Guajardo and Guajardo (2008) describe how ethnographers affiliated with the Llano Grande Center for Research and Development taught ethnographic research techniques to students in a South Texas high school. Students learned about methods of interviewing, observing, and analyzing data, and also read works on border histories, resistance narratives, culturally responsive pedagogy, and selected ethnographic studies. They then conducted research projects where they interviewed family members, neighbors, and other people in order to raise awareness about the sociocultural realities of the surrounding community. They became activist researchers and much more engaged in their own schooling.

Other strategies stem from critical ethnography leading to praxis-based pedagogy. Critical ethnography as a research approach is propelled by an ethical commitment to uncover and ameliorate injustices within particular settings. Critical ethnographers with such a commitment take us beneath surface appearances, and bring to light obscure operations of power and control in order to disrupt the status quo (Madison, 2005). They have political agendas for cultural productions aimed at fostering educational change at the local level of lived experience.

Critical school ethnographers in their fieldwork excavate the latent cultural beliefs, norms, and values that perpetuate unequal power relations. They may then work to empower students, teachers, and other school actors through what Cammarota (2008) terms *cultural organizing* leading to praxis-based pedagogy. Cultural organizing may involve cultural therapy and also critical literacy strategies such as those pioneered by Paulo Freire (1970/1993) who taught oppressed students how to read through the reading of their own sociocultural worlds and the hidden injustices within them. Cultural production via such cultural organizing strategies requires the direct involvement of ethnographic researchers and school actors who engage in critical analyses of their own local contexts with conscious attention to political dynamics; produce knowledge from their analyses for pedagogical purposes; and create cultural products for social transformation transmitted through organizations of constituents and stakeholders dedicated to creating more just and equitable schooling processes (Cammarota, 2008).

While such approaches have contributed to the production of more constructive cultural processes in rural schools such as those in South Texas, they are much more difficult to implement in urban public high schools where political dynamics can be more complex and contentious. Foundational insights into urban educational politics and policies at national, state, district, and local school levels are key to understanding how schooling in the United States works, or does not work, and how urban public high schools can or ought to be changed.

Summation

Educational anthropologists study cultural processes and how they shape education and the schooling experiences of students, teachers, administrators, and other school actors. Culture is defined as symbolic forms of meaning, or tool kits, that people configure into solutions to perennial human problems and the exigencies of everyday life. Symbolic forms coalesce into patterned strategies of action that groups of people use in their own particular adaptations to the circumstances within which they find themselves.

Urban public high schools, like all high schools, are characterized by a cultural milieu that reaffirms the "mainstream" cultural commitments of dominant

Anglo/European American, middle-class groups. Schools are widely expected to transmit this culture, and related academic curriculum, to young people regardless of their natal cultural backgrounds. They do so by facilitating processes of enculturation (where students become competent in the surrounding mainstream culture) and through acculturation (where students embracing different cultures change or sustain their commitments during ongoing contact).

Urban high schools are also sites for cultural identity work. There is interplay in this work between individuals' innermost psychocultural self and external cultural pressures. Student identity work involves the formation of academic identities against the backdrop of what it means to be, and talk and behave like an educated person in the United States. Students with strong academic identities are much more likely to accommodate to mainstream schooling than those who do not. Explicating student cultural identity work and its implications for academic identity formation is therefore important for understanding why students do what they do.

Academic achievement gaps among racial and ethnic minority high school students have persisted for decades. There has been a processional line of theories attempting to explain these gaps, which began in the 1960s with cultural deficit theory and evolved over time through the scholarship of educational anthropologists into increasingly more nuanced explanations focusing on home–school cultural discontinuities; cultural pluralism in the context of increasing urbanization; cultural ecology in light of historical discrimination against involuntary racial and ethnic minority groups; and racial formation involving racialized groups engaged in relational politics in multiracial and multiethnic settings.

Theories focusing on academic achievement gaps often pay little attention to the critical roles that teachers and other school actors play in school cultural processes. Contemporary educational anthropologists are recognizing the involvement of all school actors, especially teachers, and are reenvisioning school cultural processes as cultural productions carried out in local school settings. These productions can lead to the construction of more meaningful and empowering pedagogies through various strategies such as cultural therapy and those related to cultural organizing developed by critical ethnographers. The ultimate ideal is to generate praxis-based pedagogies that foster more just and equitable schooling processes.

Anthropological Perspectives

Discussion Questions

1. Public high schools in the United States from an anthropological perspective are expected to facilitate processes of enculturation and acculturation in ways that reaffirm "mainstream" Anglo/European American middle-class culture. Are these processes right for public high schools located in multiracial and multiethnic urban districts? Why or why not?
2. Construct a portrait of what you think the characteristics of the "educated person" ought to be in the United States.
3. Think about yourself or someone you know who has experienced difficulties adapting to high school culture and analyze them in terms of cultural theories.
4. Is it feasible for teachers and students to engage in praxis-based pedagogies? If so, then how might they go about it in multiracial and multiethnic urban public high schools? If not, then what are the barriers preventing them from doing so?

4

POLITICAL INSIGHTS

Politics of Public Education

Public schools serve the public interest, but they are also regarded by individuals, groups, and organizations as prime sites for promoting their own vested educational interests. The adage "knowledge is power" plays out in political wrangling over what the content of public school curriculum ought to be; who should make that determination; and how and which students should be taught it. How schools are funded is also hotly contested as taxpayers, corporations, and other people judge the value and outcomes of their monetary investments in public education. How, and who, should control and run public schools is also of utmost political importance.

Many people with interests in public education attempt to assert power over, and within, public schools. They vie for political influence within national, state, regional, district, and local arenas over educational initiatives and control of school operations. Such politics are especially consequential for urban public high schools where politics can be quite contentious.

National Political Arena

Ideology

Educational politics within national arenas are more matters of ideology than practicalities. Liberals, conservatives, and special interest groups at the national level are embroiled in ideological battles over public education, and promote their agendas with limited empirical grounding in, or first-hand experience with, the practical needs and realities of public schools.

Ideologies are belief systems or storylines that groups spin about the historical past, present conditions, and what the future ought to hold especially for

---

CONCEPT BOX 4.1

Ideology

Ideologies are storylines that groups spin about the historical past, present conditions, and what the future ought to hold. They are saturated with group interests.

---

them. They are saturated with group interests, and usually promoted in oppositional contrast to, or in spite of, the interests of other groups.

The educational ideologies that have the most sway at the national level are those propagated by the leadership of the Democratic and Republican Parties. Democratic and Republican legislators have considerable say over federal initiatives related to public education. And yet, they are not held directly accountable for the policies they impose, the legislation they pass, or the federal mandates they decree. As national politicians, they are remote and removed from the day-to-day operations of public schools. They have nevertheless positioned themselves as stewards of public education in ways that hold other people, most notably school administrators and teachers, directly accountable for policies and mandates over which they have little or no say. They assert power from afar over public schools in a manner that diminishes the power of the local people who run them. National educational ideologies thus necessitate examination in terms of their effects on urban public high schools.

Democratic and Republican Party Educational Ideologies

There are historical differences between educational ideologies endorsed by the Democratic and Republican Parties. As Joel Spring (2010) explains, a mainstay of Democratic Party ideology has been to end poverty through improved educational opportunities. The primary emphasis of the Democratic Party in the 1960s was on school desegregation and federal programs, such as Head Start and Upward Bound, associated with President Lyndon Johnson's War on Poverty. Ideological shifts occurred in the 1970s when White Democrats in the South deserted the party and became Republicans because of forced busing of students to achieve school integration. Although mandatory busing was a consequence of Supreme Court rulings that began with the 1954 U.S. Supreme Court ruling *Brown vs. Board of Education*, Southern voters associated such remedies with Democrats.

In response to voter flight, Democrats began to deemphasize desegregation and promote equality between racial groups in school achievement. Their rhetoric was also modified by the "culture wars" Republicans waged in the 1980s to win support for the conservative ideological belief that the

United States should be a society rooted in common Anglo/European American traditions. Republicans opposed bilingual education, promoted English-only education policies, and insisted that public school curriculum focus on Western European history, philosophy, and literature. Democrats leaned more heavily toward a vision of the United States as a multicultural society, and supported federal legislation for bilingual education, including the maintenance of languages other than English, and have been much more amenable to a multicultural curriculum.

New Democrats in the 1990s tried to attract middle-class voters through the promotion of quality education and preschool programs aimed at improving all children's chances to compete in the global economy. They also hitched their long-held ideological commitment to closing school achievement gaps to higher standards and accountability. As Spring (2010) explains:

> Standards and accountability were to help attain equality of educational opportunity. By "standards" was meant federal or state curriculum requirements for what is to be learned in class. In the language of the day, high standards meant that the federal or state governments would require students to learn increased amounts in class. "Accountability" referred to tests that would measure whether or not students had learned what the standards required. (Spring, 2010, p. 34)

CONCEPT BOX 4.2

Ideological Value Differences
Republican and Democratic Party Education Agendas

Republican	*Democratic*
Traditional American patriotism and values	Multiculturalism
English-only	Bilingual
States rights	Federal protection of civil rights
Pro-life and abstinence	Pro-choice and family planning
Traditional marriage	Supports gay/lesbian marriage and gay rights
Creationism (some Republicans)	Evolution is not a political issue

---

Republicans in the 1990s had what Spring (2010) describes as a "master political narrative" with assertions that:

- Republicans protect traditional American values
- Republicans protect traditional religious faith and values
- Poverty is the result of poor character and every American has the chance to be financially successful through hard work
- Republicans protect the free market and rely on the "invisible hand" of the market
- Republicans protect individual freedom from regulation by big government. (Spring, 2010, p. 88)

They, too, jumped on the standards and accountability bandwagon while keeping up their own ideological push for socially conservative educational programs.

In the 2000s, ideological overlaps between the two parties became more pronounced. They were rooted in human capital economic theory premised on the belief that investment in education will improve America's ability to compete in global markets, reduce unemployment, and especially important for Democrats, provide equality of opportunity. This belief coupled with shared ideological positions on standards and accountability led to bipartisan support for, and passage of No Child Left Behind (NCLB; 2001) legislation. NCLB was intended to improve public education and ensure equality in educational opportunity by exposing all children to the same curriculum. States were required to establish curricular standards; institute standardized testing to measure student achievement; issue report cards for schools; close achievement gaps; and restructure or close failing schools.

NCLB legislation and other federal initiatives identified public high schools as key to economic progress. Students are viewed as investments, and school curriculum is the raw material (educational input) of academic achievement measured through standardized testing (school output). Urban public high schools have become increasingly vulnerable as a result of these political pressures. Good teachers are much harder to retain because of the constraints testing has placed on them. Low-income urban students of color are more likely to be earmarked as underachievers and held back in school because of low standardized test scores. Schools located in impoverished inner-city neighborhoods are more at risk of being closed or overhauled. And the multiracial and multiethnic contexts of many urban high schools are virtually ignored. The impact of such legislation has repercussions for the agendas of teacher unions.

Teacher Unions

There are two major teacher unions representing public school teachers that play a crucial role in national policy and legislative debates. The largest union, the National Education Association (NEA), is an independent federation of state professional associations with approximately 2.7 million members. The American Federation of Teachers (AFT) has a membership of around 1.3 million and is affiliated with the AFL-CIO. While the AFT is also organized in state units, it is more fundamentally comprised of large urban locals (Henderson, 2004).

The main agenda for both unions is to protect teachers' rights and advance teacher compensation and benefits. The NEA and AFT, Johnson (2004) observes, are regarded by many people as having a "paralysis perspective" driven by self-interested quests for good salaries and benefits, teacher-controlled workplace policies, and job security. An alternative view, the "possibilities perspective," sees union activities as part of an overall effort to professionalize teaching and protect union members from unfair or arbitrary treatment. The two unions from the vantage point of their own perspectives wield considerable influence.

The NEA and AFT at the national level were in league with the Democratic Party drawing much criticism from Republicans who accused them of being too liberal in terms of the promotion of minority rights, antimerit pay contracts, and prolabor legislation. There was a notable shift in the 1990s when it became politically expedient for both unions to adopt more bipartisan agendas and approaches. The NEA in particular made a conscious attempt to move away from partisan politics toward the adoption of strategies aimed at electing both Democrats and Republicans who favored public education (Shust & Lewis, 2004). This union toned down its partisan rhetoric during the Bush administration (2000–2008), and engaged in outreach to Republican policymakers though voter polling and the establishment of a much stronger presence at Republican political gatherings. The NEA's legislative priorities were redirected toward better federal funding, more support for special education, and opposition to voucher plans.

The NEA and AFT have also been reshaping their images into that of reform-minded partners. They are making an effort to work with school boards to implement school-based decision making, peer reviews, professional development, performance pay policies, and other reforms (Henderson, Urban, & Wolman, 2004). But many local union chapters are viewed as hindering or sabotaging reform. This is especially true in urban public school districts where many unions have hamstrung principals with their collective bargaining victories.

Teacher unions in many urban districts have fostered a virtual tyranny of seniority by wresting significant management power away from building principals. Contracts have given senior teachers substantial authority over the schools, grade levels, and tracks to which they are assigned (Payne, 2008). The result in many urban public high schools is that the least prepared and experienced teachers are being assigned to the most needy and challenging students. Contracts have also established procedures for hiring, firing, and transferring teachers that have made it extremely difficult for principals to remove incompetent and incorrigible instructors. Unions' unbending enforcement of senior teachers' prerogatives in many districts has caused effective teachers with less seniority to be "bumped" out of their positions by teachers with more seniority regardless of their performance. It is not unusual for teaching vacancies to be filled by teachers who were not chosen by schools, including teachers that principals do not want in their building.

While there may be much to criticize about union contracts that foster a tyranny of seniority, it is also the case that unions in many urban districts have to deal with the stark realities of high teacher turnover, poor working conditions, insufficient resources, and students in dire need of support beyond what teachers can realistically provide. The NEA and AFT are understandably protective of teachers in these situations. But they also need to be more proactive players in urban school reform. Henderson et al. (2004) suggest that:

> [T]hey … gather more information on effective reforms; develop greater internal consensus for reform; devise strategies to overcome constraints in the legal and contractual system of education; and make the case for adequate and fair commitment and distribution of resources to education. [They should] work cooperatively and productively with legislatures, school districts, parents, communities, and students. If these groups take joint accountability for our education system, we have a good chance at building that system in ways that enhance the teaching profession as well as the equity and quality of students' educational experience. (p. xiv)

These recommendations would certainly move the NEA and AFT toward a perspective with greater possibilities, but none of these recommendations is likely to come to fruition without addressing the complex, somewhat byzantine nature of regional, district, and ultimately school level micropolitics.

Regional and District Political Arenas

The politics of urban public high schools at regional and district levels are notably affected by top-down federal initiatives and union agendas. But they are also shaped by demographic forces, issues related to school financing, and the micropolitics of district central offices, school boards, teacher unions, and partnering organizations. Urban school districts serve the most demographically diverse students in the country. Many are divided into residential areas where low-income and working-class families of color are clustered in inner-city neighborhoods isolated from more advantaged groups living in the outer edges. The most smoothly functioning schools are those with close ties to, and the full support of, the local communities they serve. This is not always the case for urban high schools serving inner-city youths living in insular and economically depressed neighborhoods that are disconnected from public institutions and other parts of the city.

Related to demographics is the fact that financial support for public schools rests on the ability and willingness of citizens to fund them. Schools are supported by property taxes and state aid allocated in accordance with legislated formulas that are supposed to be equitable. But because the tax base in impoverished inner-city districts is low, and states in recent years have experienced significant decreases in revenue, urban public high schools are dealing with severe budget cuts. They are drastically underfunded and in desperate need of other sources of revenue.

Budgetary challenges are compounded and worsened by insidious micropolitics. Rather than work together toward mutually and educationally acceptable goals, central offices, school boards, and teacher unions often vie for or abuse power. Rogers (1969) in his eye-opening account of politics and bureaucracy in New York City describes a paralyzing condition of checkmated power that is eerily similar to what is happening in many large urban public school districts today. Power struggles are so intense, and separation between hierarchically bloated offices is so wide, that it is not clear who has or should have the power to get things done.

As if checkmate politics are not bad enough, many urban school districts are plagued with backstabbing, graft, financial mismanagement, and out-and-out crime and corruption. Paychecks in New Orleans have been issued to people who should not have been paid; a union leader in Washington, DC was sent to prison for her role in setting up a professional development business where she and other union officials siphoned off money into their own pockets; and school boards in other cities are forums for politicians to lobby for pet projects (Payne, 2008).

Self-interested micropolitical activities can be aggravated or ameliorated by institutions of higher education, corporations, industries, businesses, community agencies, and other organizations. Such organizations come into political play through multi-institutional partnerships forged at regional and district levels and also at the level of individual schools. Partnering organizations may have a common interest in improving urban high schools, but they also have special interests related to their own organizational aims. Common and special interests are realized through logics of sociopolitical relations deeply entrenched in organizational cultures.

Logics of Sociopolitical Relations

The *logics* of sociopolitical relations in multi-institutional partnerships are the norms, values, and beliefs that shape the actions and interactions of organizational actors as they vie for control over the means, aims, and resources associated with educational initiatives. These logics have a significant bearing on what people from different organizations regard as the most appropriate social and political roles for them to play; how they should behave as sociopolitical actors; and whether or how they should assert or acquiesce to political power and authority. Each organization has its own logics of sociopolitical relations that are "logical" given their interests and cultural patterns for attaining and exercising power and securing and utilizing resources.

The logics of sociopolitical relations in urban public high schools are very much influenced by their variable goals, uncertain technologies, semibureaucratic structures, and unstable authority relations. Urban high school administrators, teachers, and students can be embroiled in messy internal politics that are affected to some extent by external forces including those that involve organizational partners with their own distinctive sociopolitical logics. Among these partners are universities, colleges, and other institutions of higher education (IHE).

Faculty members in IHEs are usually the people most directly involved in multi-institutional partnerships involving high schools. Within IHEs, especially Research I universities, faculty members are somewhat removed from upper-level administration and expected to be entrepreneurial, especially with regards to research activities (Slater, 1996). Their organizational roles are fluid and subject to change. They can be mainly teachers, researchers with few teaching responsibilities, administrators, or assume other roles over the course of their careers (Hoffman-Johnson, 2007). Their social position and political power reside in their expertise. It is not uncommon for IHE faculty members to exude their expertise and experience in efforts to assert their power and influence especially in decision-making processes.

The logics of IHE faculty sociopolitical relations are rooted in modes of autonomous and decentralized governance that are notoriously inefficient ways to establish and achieve goals. Faculty members in their decision making engage in deliberations that can confound, prolong, or stall outcomes. They jockey for dominance in relation to their colleagues, and sometimes in their interactions with high school teachers and administrators. This can ignite social and political friction.

The sociopolitical logics of urban high schools and IHEs may also rub up against the more purely bureaucratic, top-down logics of corporations, industries, and businesses. Corporations, industries, and businesses usually have more clearly defined goals achieved through specified tasks, timelines, and other

rationalized means. Decision making is top-down in accordance with institutionalized procedures and rules. And outcomes are tangible and measurable.
The sociopolitical logics that emanate from these organizational cultures clash
with those of high schools and IHEs. The clash can generate or fuel tensions in
multi-institutional partnership relations. Whether or how logics are reconciled
affects the ways that individuals and groups manage to work together. True
collaboration is the most ideal form of multi-institutional and, for that matter,
internal school sociopolitical relations. But it is difficult to realize, and usually
supplanted by other types of sociopolitical relations.

Collaboration

Collaboration is often touted, indeed extolled as key to the success of urban
high school educational reform and innovative change. The most ideal collaborations are those where people have tight-knit social relations and egalitarian
political arrangements that accentuate common interests, address special interests, promote the best interests of educators and students, and encourage everyone to work together in an equitable manner. Such collaborations depend on
logics of sociopolitical relations that make it possible for different people with
different interests to work together toward the realization of mutually agreed
upon outcomes. They are characterized by power sharing where no individual,
group, or organization dominates or controls another. And they rest on a great
deal of mutual trust and identification with others involved in the endeavor
(Kuh & Whitt, 1998; Slater, 1996).

Unfortunately, ideal collaborations, especially in multi-institutional urban
public high school partnerships, are not easily forged much less sustained. People must transcend the bounded worlds of their internal school or external
organizational cultural frames of reference. They have to be willing to engage
in what Slater (1996) describes as constructive "culture creating" where organizations and people "come together to create something new and in the process
create a new form of sustainable collaboration" (p. 49). While the construction
of culturally blended and democratic forms of collaboration is ideal, the reality
is that such collaborations are very hard to create in urban public high school
contexts where the logics of sociopolitical relations are notably and sometimes
intractably divergent. Mutual trust, common interests, and transgroup identification can be extremely difficult to achieve, and ongoing tensions over power,
authority, and control are ever-present and not easily mediated.

Time is another complicating factor. During the school year teachers and
school administrators cannot meet together on a regular basis much less with
external institutional partners. IHE faculty members decide how much time
they will devote to educational initiatives. Corporations, industries, and business have their own schedules which may or may not be conducive for ongoing
collaborative interactions with urban high school personnel and IHE faculty.

CONCEPT BOX 4.3

Sociopolitical Relations

Collaboration is a tight-knit social and egalitarian political arrangement that accentuates common interests, recognizes special interests, promotes the best interests of educators and students, and encourages everyone to work together in an equitable manner.

Alliances are temporary arrangements formed by people with shared interests in particular, short-term endeavors.

Networks exist for the exchange of information and ideas. They are nonconfrontational, informal, sometimes antiestablishment, and may include people with no social capital or political power.

Cooperation is a low-level work arrangement where people go along with ideas and may contribute some time and effort but are not deeply vested.

Bounded factions arise from the competing agendas and interests of groups whose members erect exclusive social boundaries and vie for status, resources, and power.

Antagonistic opposition emerges when groups become locked in conflict marred by hostilities.

The result is that not enough shared time is spent on collaborative educational endeavors.

The ideal sociopolitical relations and time that make collaboration possible are fraught with challenges. Because of that, other types of sociopolitical relations usually come into play.

Other Types of Sociopolitical Relations

There are other more common types of sociopolitical relations with logics that affect multi-institutional partnerships. They include alliances, networks, cooperation, bounded factions, and antagonistic opposition. *Alliances* are temporary social arrangements formed by people with shared interests; in particular, short-term endeavors. They dissolve when objectives are achieved or thwarted. *Networks* facilitate the exchange of information and ideas and are tapped into when people need some sort of assistance from others. They are nonconfrontational; bypass institutional formality; are sometimes antiestablishment; and can involve people with no social capital or political power (Slater, 1996). Although networks are pervasive, they are not necessarily conducive for ensuring that tasks are performed and change occurs. *Cooperation* represents a low-level form of joint work where groups attempt to fulfill short-term goals, and people are willing to contribute some of their time and effort to a project. The individuals involved may not be deeply vested in, or inclined to stick with, cooperative efforts for long durations. *Bounded factions* arise when groups with competing agendas and interests are formed and members erect exclusive social boundaries. Factions vie with one another for status, resources, and power. *Antagonistic opposition* emerges when competing groups become locked in conflict marred by hostilities that may be so fierce that partnerships and school communities are torn apart.

The reality of sociopolitical relations and the logics that drive them is that power, influence, authority, and control are constantly contested and seized as collaborations work or do not work; alliances form, realign, or dissolve; network information flows, shifts, and ebbs; cooperation waxes and wanes; and factions and antagonistic opposition flare up and die down. This happens at all levels of educational politics, but is most consequential at the everyday school level as administrators, teachers, and students engage in the politics of everyday life in offices, classrooms, and corridors.

Everyday Politics in Classrooms and Corridors

School-Level Governance

There are different models of school-level governance structures. The most traditional are ones where principals assert their power and authority as bosses at the top, and are served by teachers and other employees lower down in the organizational hierarchy. Other models are characterized by forms of shared governance where principals and teachers work together to set policy, establish goals, manage programs, and perform other administrative tasks. Traditional hierarchical pyramids are essentially turned upside down (Page & Wong, 2000). And principals assume more servant leadership roles where their highest priority is meeting the needs of students, teachers, and other school personnel. Rather than being served, the emphasis is on service to others; fostering a sense of community; shared decision making; and the creation of a more open school climate (Greenleaf, 1991).

Other models of governance are centered on teacher leadership. In 1986, the Carnegie Corporation released a report, *A Nation Prepared: Teachers for the Twenty-first Century,* which lent support to a growing movement to reinvigorate and professionalize teaching by positioning K–12 teachers as school leaders. The report argued that teachers should take the lead in curriculum, instruction, school and program redesign, and professional development, and be given "real power" to improve student achievement (Lieberman & Miller, 2004, p. 8). Among the most effective teacher leadership or teacher-led governance structures are those that include instructional teams where teachers work together, rather than in isolation, to develop and implement best practices.

School-level governance however it is structured ultimately depends on the nature and quality of social relationships. Bryk and Schneider (2002) in their groundbreaking research make a strong case for recognizing and addressing *relational trust* as crucial if not essential for running and improving schools. Relational trust, organized around sets of role relationships, is key to whether or how teachers can obtain and make use of external support, professional development, and other means to deliver best practices. As Bryk and Schneider (2002) explain:

> Relational trust is organized around a distinct set of role relationships: Teachers with students, teachers with other teachers, teachers with parents and with their school principal. Each party in a role relationship maintains an understanding of his or her role obligations and holds some expectations about the role obligations of others. (p. 20)

Relational trust breaks down when individuals perceive that the people they are working with are not behaving in ways consistent with their role obligations. Trust very much depends on what behaviors people observe, and whether these behaviors are interpreted as being consistent with expectations associated with role responsibilities and relations.

The four criteria for discerning appropriate behaviors most conductive for building relational trust are *respect, competence, personal regard for others*, and *integrity*. Respect in schools involves the recognition that each person is playing an important role in students' education, and to make schooling work everyone involved is mutually dependent. There is a positive feeling of esteem for administrators, teachers, students, and parents, and genuine listening where everyone's perspective is taken into account.

CONCEPT BOX 4.4

Criteria for Relational Trust

Respect is the recognition that each person is playing an important role; is mutually dependent on one another; is esteemed; and is listened to.

Competence is the ability to execute role responsibilities in a manner that achieves desired goals.

Personal regard for others is feeling and conveying care for colleagues, students, and others.

Integrity is consistency between what people say and do guided by moral–ethical perspectives.

Competence has to do with the execution of individuals' role responsibilities. A competent person is able and willing to achieve desired outcomes. People who are incompetent are unable to meet goals or they undermine the work of others. Gross incompetence is corrosive to trust relations.

Personal regard for others is fostered when people feel that others care about them. Teachers, for example, who truly care about colleagues and students, may stay extra hours after the school day to work on program improvements, meet with parents, or get involved in community activities.

The last criterion, integrity, is apparent when there is consistency between what people say and what they actually do. It is also perceived when a moral–ethical perspective appears to be guiding a person's actions. When all is said and done, "actions [in schools] must be understood as … advancing the interest of children" rather than the self (selfish) interests of employees (Bryk & Schneider, 2002, p. 26). Integrity in this sense is a moral resource that strengthens relational trust.

When there is little or no relational trust, conflicts arise and politically volatile battles inevitably ensue. Unfortunately, as Weiner (2006) has observed, mistrust in role relations is common in urban public schools, especially between teachers and administrators, and it can incite a kind of warfare.

> In most urban schools, a kind of warfare exists between teachers and their supervisors. The battle can be a guerrilla operation in which both sides continually snipe or, less frequently, all–out–war. In either case, relations are generally strained and hostile. (p. 49)

Warfare also occurs in classrooms albeit in ways that often involve a fair amount of playful gamesmanship.

Classroom Politics: Ecology of Games

Classrooms are also political arenas where teachers determine academic achievement hierarchies as part of their official duties. Classroom dynamics are politically more manageable for teachers when students accept achievement hierarchies. But if criteria for achievement rankings do not make sense or are applied erroneously or unfairly, then students will rearrange the political situation in a fashion that is more commiserate with their own perceived statuses and abilities. They will produce their own sociopolitical hierarchies that counter those of the teacher.

Teachers and students within their respective hierarchical arrangements become players in what Long (1958) described long ago as an *ecology of games*. Far from being outdated, the notion of game ecologies in institutions like schools is an enduring and widely recognizable way to explain how everyday politics work. People by nature are game-playing and game-creating animals who use game metaphors to describe their work and other activities involv-

CONCEPT BOX 4.5

Classroom Ecology of Games

Classroom ecologies of games give teachers and students a sense of purpose, identities, and roles they can play out in engrossing, dramatic, and entertaining ways in front of real or generalized spectators, presumably keeping score.

ing other people. Games, or some semblance of games, give people a sense of purpose, identity, and roles they can play out in front of real or generalized spectators who are presumably keeping score. These games can be dramatic, entertaining, or all-engrossing in ways that add to their appeal.

Different games with different ecological structures are played in schools and other organizations. People who play the games "know how to behave, and know the score" because they know the rules of the game that structure them (Long, 1958, p. 253). Good players win coveted prizes, desired goods, and social acceptance. They also garner power and dominance in their everyday relations. Politically, they are on top of their games.

Urban public high school administrators, teachers, students, and staff occupy a territorial field where they play their everyday political games. McDermott (1974), who applied the ecology of games concept in his studies of urban classrooms, found that students playing the achievement game within teachers' ecologies have to follow directions, complete homework assignments, study for tests, and accept all of the statuses and judgments of ability that go along with these and other actions. If for some reason they cannot or will not follow teachers' rules of the game, they will come up with their own countergames where they intentionally ignore or thwart teachers' orders, reject curricular materials, and otherwise "learn how not to learn" (McDermott, 1974, p.112). Students who play countergames well achieve high status and other social benefits in relation to their peers, but they also achieve school failure. They win classroom matches in the short run, but lose educational tournaments in the long run.

In urban high school classrooms, especially those serving large numbers of disaffected racial and ethnic minority youths, everyday politics may escalate into what McDermott terms "war games." In such situations, teachers' ecology of games clash with students' games, and which games ultimately prevail determines how power is distributed and who gets to exercise it.

Clashes can occur in any classroom, including Advanced Placement (AP) and other classes that are supposed to be academically rigorous. An example is an AP English class I observed in an urban high school (Hemmings, 2003). The teacher, Ms. Thomas, began the class by instructing students to write an essay based on a sample AP exam question. Students were to pick a book from a list of literary classics and write about a character whose brief appearance had a profound impact on the plot. She provided the example of King Hamlet whose fleeting appearance as a ghost set off the dramatic chain of events in Shakespeare's play *Hamlet*. A few students wrote some sentences, stopped writing to talk with friends, wrote a few more sentences, and then spent the rest of the time talking to their friends. Some did not write at all. They simply conversed with their friends. There was only one student in the class who worked on the essay with no social interaction.

Ms. Thomas decided to take control of the situation. She issued orders. "Please listen to me," she told the class in a stern voice. "I'm the teacher, okay? Be quiet and listen up." Then she asked students if they had found an example of a character. A girl blurted out that she was "going to do the guy who raped that girl in *The Color Purple*." She proceeded to describe the rape scene in graphic, somewhat embellished detail. Students laughed uproariously as Ms. Thomas stood in stunned silence. The girl used a game tactic that utterly deflated the teacher's power. The tactic was especially effective because it was within the bounds of the teacher's instructions. The rape scene in *The Color Purple* was brief yet profoundly significant for the story's plot. Ms. Thomas was resoundingly defeated by her own rules of the games.

The winners of classroom games move to the top of the social hierarchy. They become the recognized leaders who run subsequent plays. What happens during the entire length of a game may be beneficial for both teachers and students. But prevailing game ecologies may also incite ongoing classroom war scenes where there are no clear winners and many losers.

Teacher and student games are not always or necessarily in opposition. They can be virtually the same or blended in ways that result in mutually acceptable compromises, and compromises quell contentiousness. But they can also result in educationally debilitating settlements. Students in their countergames disrupt teachers' games through constant joking, refusal to complete assignments, sleeping, or other tactics. Teachers in response to the onslaught may engage in "defensive teaching" where they water down curriculum, bombard students with fill-in-the-blank worksheets, and otherwise reduce instruction "to simplistic, teacher-controlled information that requires no reading or writing by the students, little or no student discussion, and very little use of the school's resources" (McNeil, 1983, pp. 115–116). They essentially defend themselves by surrendering much if not all of their power over achievement criteria.

Some teachers go on the offensive. They are masters at establishing their authority and winning student compliance. They have exceptional teaching skills and a willingness to go the extra mile in the face of daunting obstacles. Urban public school teachers have to work harder and have better teaching skills to achieve the same degree of success they would have in environments that do not undercut their efforts (Weiner, 2006). Not only do they need exceptional teaching skills, they also need the kind of political savvy that will enable them to assert their authority over students.

Everyday politics also play out in corridors. Political success in these locations very much depends on whether or how students harness power in relation to peers, especially the power of respect.

Corridor Politics: The Power of Respect

Students spend about an hour in hallways, lunchrooms, bathrooms, and other corridor spaces. This hour, less than 1/6th of the scheduled school day, is vibrant and alive with highly consequential student political performances. Students are in charge of what happens during this hour. Teachers, security guards, and other school staff may be present, but they generally do not intervene in the maelstrom of corridor life unless events get out of hand.

My first impression of corridor life in a study I conducted on the "hidden corridor curriculum" of an urban high school was that it was chaotic (Hemmings, 2000a). Hallways were crowded with teenagers leaning against lockers, walking or running in various directions, and sitting with friends on stairs and floors eating candy bars, potato chips, and other snack foods. Lovers held each other in passionate embraces. Adversaries exchanged fleeting punches, dirty looks, or verbal insults. All of this was carried out in a deafening din of loud talking, laughter, and arguing. There appeared to be little order to corridor sights and sounds. But with time I began to discern deeply entrenched sociopolitical patterns structuring student actions and interactions.

Students upon closer inspection were divided into cliques mostly along strict racial, ethnic, and gender lines. The cliques had names. There were White, working-class boys known as "skinheads," "head bangers," and "grunge." Some Black male students were referred to as "playas" and their female counterparts were "fly girls" or "hoochies." There were "gangbangers" who belonged to real or pseudo street gangs with names like "City Boyz," "Gangsters with Drama," and "Forest Hill Posse." And there were "normal" kids who did their best to blend into the corridor scene without calling attention to themselves. Social divisions were most apparent in lunchrooms where cliques sat around separate, territorially well-defined tables.

Cliques had their own language and dress codes. Some of them had members who spoke neighborhood dialects, others communicated in Standard English. Almost all of them loaded their speech with the latest teenage slang, occasionally punctuated with profanity. Skinheads shaved their heads and sported tattoos. Gangbangers wore clothes with special colors and insignia indicating their gang affiliations. Kids in other cliques donned apparel that set them off in their own socially symbolic ways.

There were also starkly divisive social borders between cliques. Skinheads were described as being like "Nazis" because, as one girl explained, "they hate Blacks, Jews, and everybody else except bad-ass White boys like themselves." Black youths projected images of coolness that sent signals to Whites and other kids that they were tough and should not be messed with.

It also became evident during the course of my study that students were engaging in everyday corridor politics that were intended to build up, and tear down, social hierarchies in quests for status and power. Corridor politics in many urban public high schools are played out in contests between teenagers jockeying for dominance or protection from domination. Respect in these contests is an enormously valuable if not essential social commodity. It is the symbolic capital urban youths must have to survive. Winning respect is necessary for asserting, challenging, or blockading domination. To lose respect is to become powerless, subordinate, and vulnerable to abuse.

There are different strategies urban youth use to win and keep respect. Gordon (1997) identifies two of them in what he describes as the opposing twin discourses of respectability and reputation. Focusing in particular on young Black men, he traces the discursive roots of respectability to the patriarchal cultural practices of African traditions and codes of mainstream, middle-class propriety. A Black man seeking respectability adopts conservative styles of dress and deportment, and adheres to the conservative values of "hard work, economic frugality and independence, community commitment and activism, mutual help and uplift, personal responsibility [and] religious faith" (p. 41). He also adopts the elaborated speech codes of Standard English.

Reputation, in marked contrast, is acquired by standing up to authorities, showing up male rivals, and controlling women. It is also attained by adopting street talk. Black male teenagers who want to build up their reputations may also follow what Anderson (1998) refers to as the code of the streets. This code arises in places where the influence of police, teachers, and other adult authority figures end and where personal responsibility for one's safety and socioeconomic advancement begins. Among the main features of the code are verbal expressions of disrespect toward competitors or people who come off as easy prey. Disrespect is also shown by stealing another person's possessions, messing with someone's woman, pulling a trigger, or tearing people apart with slashing insults. If a man loses his reputation, he loses respect. If he loses respect, he must regain it even if he has to get into fistfights or resort to other forms of violent retaliation.

Young men from other ethnic groups also seek the power of respect by cultivating images of respectability and reputation. Young women do the same often with the added burden of defending themselves against male sexual predation. Many of them, as Adams (1999) observed in her research, engage in a sexual politics that simultaneously position them as docile and not-so-docile female bodies. They make a concerted effort to force disrespectful boys to maintain more respectful relations with them while, at the same time, projecting images as tough girls with reputations for being just as capable as boys of asserting dominance through physical strength, aggression, and fearless counterattacks. They also fight for respect.

Physical fights for respect in urban public high school corridors are common and often staged as planned performances. Most contests for respect are not, however, performed in full public display. They are more often than not hidden from view and rarely reported to adults. And they can cause irreparable harm to individual students and intergroup relations.

Summation

Politics permeate urban public high school policy, legislation, and operations from the national level on down into classrooms and corridors. Federal initiatives at the national level are saturated with ideological differences and convergences promulgated by Democratic and Republican Parties. Historically, Democrats have taken liberal stances on equal educational opportunity, multiculturalism, bilingualism, and preschool programs, while Republicans have upheld traditional Anglo and Western European curriculum, English-only policies, school choice, and conservative social agendas. Both parties in recent years supported legislation, most notably No Child Left Behind, intended to raise standards and ensure accountability primarily through standardized testing. Neither political party is held directly accountable for the outcomes of their initiatives.

Teacher unions, especially the NEA and AFT, are also part of the national scene. Their primary agenda is to protect teachers' rights, advance teacher compensation, and secure teacher benefits. Both unions for many years were allied with the Democratic Party. But they became more bipartisan in the 1980s when Republicans began to seize more control over educational agendas. They are currently stepping up efforts to be more directly involved in school reform including reform of urban public high schools. But these efforts are inevitably affected by the politics of local school districts and regional institutions of higher education, corporations, and industries.

Politics at the district and regional level are guided by the logics of sociopolitical relations embedded in organizational cultures. Logics can clash between urban high schools and external organizations with divergent interests in public education. Collaborations involving interorganizational partnerships are ideal. But political activities in reality usually take place through alliances, networks, temporary cooperation, bounded factions, or antagonistic opposition. The dynamics of relations in political activities are not only critical at the district and regional level, but also, and more consequentially, at the everyday level of classrooms and corridors.

The everyday politics of urban high school classrooms play out in ecologies of games where teachers and students compete for the predominance of their particular academic and social hierarchies. Ecologies have their own rules of the game, and provide players with a sense of purpose, identity, and roles. Games are played in front of real or generalized audiences who keep score.

Teachers and students win or lose classroom games with short-term and long-run educational consequences.

Politics are also played out in corridor spaces where students vie for the power of respect in their everyday encounters. Students in urban high schools divide themselves into cliques along racial, ethnic, social class, gender, and other lines. They set themselves off through symbolically distinctive dress, language, and behavior codes. They garner and deploy respect in physical and symbolic contests for dominance. Winning respect is essential for asserting, challenging, or blocking domination. Youths who lose respect, or never had it in the first place, are extremely vulnerable and often defenseless in the face of peer abuse and attacks. Many are literally shoved to the bottom of a multilevel political hierarchy where kids like them are utterly powerless. They are the ultimate losers in urban public high schools.

Political Insights

Discussion Questions

1. Given that national Democratic and Republican legislators are not directly accountable for federal educational legislation and policies, should urban public high school initiatives be limited or confined to region, district, and local levels where accountability may be more feasible? Why or why not?
2. The NEA and AFT are becoming more politically involved in school reform efforts. What should unionized teachers working in urban public high schools negotiate over or give up to promote the success of such efforts?
3. How might urban public school districts and external organizations with divergent logics of sociopolitical relations forge ideal collaborations?
4. Urban high school classrooms are characterized by ecologies of games that can pit teachers against students. Have you experienced or observed classrooms where this has occurred? What tactics did students and teachers use? Who won? Who lost?
5. Students in urban public high school corridors engage in performances, fights, and other contests for the power of respect. What can or should school administrators, teachers, and other adults do to mediate or ameliorate these contests?

PART II

Possibilities

A familiar representation of public school reform is that there are essentially two kinds: top-down and bottom-up. Top-down reforms are activated or devised at the national level by federal, judicial, legislative, and policymaking bodies with attention to, or in spite of, the prerogatives of state departments of education and school districts. They may be instigated by court orders or initiated by members of Congress or other political figures prone to politicize public education in keeping with the ideological tenets of their political parties. Top-down reforms eventually trickle down into local schools where school administrators, teachers, and staff are expected to absorb them.

Reforms are also rendered as bottom-up affairs implemented within individual schools by school administrators and teachers, ideally with the backing of local school boards, teacher unions, and parents. Some schools adopt programs developed by outsiders while others construct their own initiatives aimed at addressing localized problems. A notion prevalent among the exponents of bottom-up reforms is that the more successful ones can be scaled up to include other schools.

Conceiving school reforms as an either–or phenomenon—as either coming from high above or arising from local depths below—is heuristically useful but also inherently problematic because it essentially construes possibilities for change as we–they processes. It is either "we" or "they" who calls the shots, and better "us" than "them." Judges, federal and state legislators, school district officials, teacher union leaders, regional external partners, superintendents, principals, teachers, parents, and many other groups with vested interests in urban public high schools can be, and often are, pitted against one another in ways that hurt rather than help students. They create or exacerbate problems and conflicts rather than solve or resolve them.

Despite the multitude of problems faced by urban public high schools, and the conflicts between groups seeking control, we can envision and implement effective possibilities for urban public high school reform, especially if we take into consideration the historical, sociological, anthropological, and political foundations of schooling. Such consideration begins with the recognition and analyses of local urban public high schools as staging areas for good instruction and authentic learning. Principals, teachers, support staff, students, parents, and external partners are crucial actors in these staging areas. They are the most practical and critical agents of change who act and interact with students each and every day. It is they, not remote judges, legislators, and policymakers who are in the best position to make a difference or make sure that nothing different happens.

Various possibilities have been attempted through past and present urban high school reforms. Most of these efforts have focused on structural, curricular, and assessment related changes. School culture, including moral order, has not been a major focus of reform despite its fundamental importance. Much can be learned from past and present urban public high school reforms, and much can be built upon and added to them. Possibilities for reform, as will become clear in the final analysis, must not only attend to better ways to restructure beleaguered urban public high schools, but also on reculturation and remoralization. Attention to restructuring, reculturation, and remoralization is the key to effective, empowering, sustainable, and practically hopeful change.

5

LOCAL SCHOOL STAGING AREAS

Setting the Stage

The historical, sociological, anthropological, and political foundations of urban public high schools set the general stage for reform possibilities. Sociologically, high schools are semibureaucratic institutions where adults and adolescents with diverse backgrounds, competing commitments, and very different individual characteristics engage in the social construction of what actually takes place in offices, classrooms, and corridors. Schools are the local staging areas where school actors—principals, teachers, support staff, and students—produce and express values, norms, beliefs, routines, rituals, standards, and other aspects of their school's organizational culture. An essential feature of this culture is the moral order that guides what actors regard as the proper, right, or only way to meet educational goals. This order is contestable, not necessarily shared, and may be demoralizing.

The social construction of schooling is structured within social systems intended to socialize adolescents into adult roles and sort them into occupational statuses. All public high schools have structures that place tight controls on credentialing processes, class scheduling, curricular topics and guidelines, assessment standards, testing procedures, graduation requirements, and other ritual classifications. They also have loosely coupled activity structures that provide school actors with some autonomy in their daily performances. The actual work of education occurs in isolated offices and classrooms that are not usually subject to direct procedural controls, close inspections, or frequent evaluations. Schooling within loosely coupled activity structures depends on trust where school actors who occupy higher levels assume that what is going on at lower levels makes sense and is actually working.

In terms of their demographics, many urban public high schools serve multiracial and multiethnic student populations with a large proportion of their clientele coming from low-income and working-class families. These schools, as has been noted by educational anthropologists, have a long history of "Americanization," which is reaffirmed in standard curriculum replete with the academic and cultural commitments of the dominant Anglo/European middle-class groups. Teachers are expected to transmit this curriculum to young people regardless of their cultural backgrounds. These expectations may be and often are resisted by racial and ethnic minority students in their cultural identity work. This is especially likely to happen among youths from groups subjected to historical discrimination.

Historians describe the enormous impact that decades of Supreme Court orders, legislation, and other federal, state, and district directives have had on urban public schools. Directives come, go, or become deeply entrenched with the historical flow of social, cultural, political, economic, judicial, legal, and legislative changes. Some, especially the desegregation of racially segregated school districts, had a highly disruptive effect on urban public high schools. Many of these schools in the aftermath of many other landmark court cases are also required to accommodate students speaking English as their second language and those with special needs. They had to adapt to these and other monumental changes regardless of whether they had the capacity, resources, and support to do so. The quality of education schools offered depended on the effectiveness of their adaptations.

Politics are an integral part of schooling at every level. National, state, and regional politics infused with the ideologies of the Democratic and Republican Parties have had a profound impact on the policies, initiatives, and legislation with ramifications for urban public high schools. Teacher unions insert their own agendas into the political fray. And there are politics at the regional and school district level that, especially when they involve institutions of higher education, businesses, and other external partners, generate a host of Byzantine political plots and power plays. At the local school site level are the micropolitics of school administrators, teachers, and students who are constantly vying for power and control. Everyone in their political maneuverings attends to the logics of sociopolitical relations in their collaborations, alliances, networks, cooperative endeavors, factions, and oppositions. Students in their stratagems are especially effective political players in the classroom ecology of games where they may win in the short run but ultimately lose in the long educational haul. What follows is a more detailed description of the roles school actors are expected to play and the pressures that can make effective role performances in urban public high schools very difficult. This discussion is followed by revealing examinations of classroom, corridor, and principal dramas.

School Actors

Principals, teachers, students, school board members, union officials, superintendents, parents, and external partners are the school actors most responsible for making sure that students are provided with good schooling. They can be effective agents of change or accessories to chronic failure. They may utilize best practices, or be complicit in ineffective administration and instruction. These actors may be constructively pragmatic in the handling of external directives. Or they can wallow in cynicism and resistance to new initiatives, policies, and mandates. All of them play important parts in how schooling is ultimately constructed, so it is imperative to understand what their roles are supposed to be and how they are actually performed in urban public high schools.

Principals

When we visualize the ideal principal it conjures up an image of a school leader who is highly respected, visible in classrooms and corridors, and has justified conceptions of what good teaching is and how students should learn and behave. He or she does an effective job of setting directions; managing daily administrative, logistical, and financial matters; providing instructional leadership; and enforcing student disciplinary, safety, and other policies. An ideal principal also manages to carry out his or her duties in the interrelational midst of district central office officials, union officers, teachers, students, and parents, and the conflicts, dilemmas, and politics such relationships entail. Ideally this leader ensures the smooth functioning of the school and is able to lead the charge for change when change is necessary. But in many urban public high schools the principal's role has become so circumscribed and overloaded that it is virtually impossible to attend to everything that the job demands.

Among the most important roles of principals is instructional leadership. But such leadership in urban public high schools can be quite daunting for a number of reasons. Mountains of paperwork, budgetary decisions and accounting, and countless other administrative minutiae make it very difficult for principals to find the time to engage faculty in conversations about instruction, provide professional development, mentor new teachers, or visit other schools to see what they are doing (Fullan, 2007). This reality is compounded by the fact that many principals find it very hard to confront ineffective or incompetent teachers. Teachers are far from being a homogeneous group and in the most troubled urban high schools are anything but one big happy family. Principals may have the formal authority to improve teachers' instruction, but their actual power to intervene is blocked by social and structural boundaries. Many of them feel there is little that can be done about what goes on inside classrooms, especially if the teacher has tenure or a lot of seniority. Union contracts place additional constraints on their ability to improve instruction. Contractual grievance procedures may be such long and drawn out quasi-judicial affairs that principals may not have the stomach to initiate them. Principals tend to avoid confrontations with teachers because they can aggravate or shatter morale. They simply do not want sustained conflict with faculty members. As Sarason (1996) explains, they want to be and to feel influential, but paralyzing dilemmas crop up with the realization that their authority, far from guaranteeing intended outcomes, may actually produce the opposite of what is desired.

> When hostility and resistance to…recommendations or ideas for change are encountered, the principal feels there is one of two alternative means of response: assert authority or withdraw from the fray. The usual consequence of either response is to widen the psychological gap and to increase the feelings of isolation of those involved. (Sarason, 1996, p. 160)

Dilemmas associated with instructional leadership are compounded by an ongoing preoccupation with violent and disruptive student behavior. Principals must deal with student discipline not only because of the need to shore up the authority of school personnel, but also because of threats to physical safety. Student-on-student fistfights, sexual harassment, robberies, and other acts of violence are common occurrences in the most troubled urban public high schools. So, too, are egregious student challenges to teachers' authority. Principals are constantly called upon to control unruly student behavior and are convenient targets of criticism if the number of fights, crimes, and other reported acts of violence is high. They may come under attack if student suspensions and expulsions are heavily skewed toward particular racial and ethnic groups. They are thus in no-win situations when it comes to student discipline.

CONCEPT BOX 5.1

Principal's Role

Ideal principals of urban public high schools are highly respected leaders who are visible in classrooms and corridors, and have justifiable conceptions of good teaching, student learning, and proper behavior. They set directions; manage daily administrative, logistical, and financial matters; provide instructional leadership; and enforce student disciplinary, safety, and other policies. They are able to carry out their duties in their relations with district central office officials, union officers, teachers, students, and parents, and can handle conflict, dilemmas, and politics. Good principals ensure the smooth functioning of their school and lead change when change is necessary.

Principals are also frequently asked by district central offices to implement directives, and to do so in ways where they have to figure out what strategies the district would like them to use. They may also have to impose directives on teachers who may not appreciate or agree with the imposition. And they have to answer to the superintendant or other district officials when directives are not carried out. Principals also have to deal with the complaints of parents who may have deep if not understandable distrust of schools. They are thus entangled in external relationships that place enormous pressure on them to follow orders and resolve conflicts, but with little or no sensitivity to what they are really up against. This can be maddening, sometimes literally.

Teachers

Urban public high school teachers play a number of roles. They are classroom instructors who typically teach over 140 students scheduled into classes differentiated by curricular content and periods. They are assigned lunch, hallway, bus, study hall, and other outside classroom duties; attend parent, committee, department, and in-service meetings; and supervise clubs, coach athletic teams, and become involved in other afterschool and extracurricular activities. Teachers may also serve as department chairs, program facilitators, or in other administrative roles. Or they may take on quasi-parenting roles such as informal student counseling or interventions involving social services.

As classroom instructors, teachers are expected to transmit specified kinds and levels of standardized curricular knowledge and skills to diverse adolescents whose sociocultural backgrounds, abilities, and interests vary immensely. And they are expected to convey curriculum in a fixed period of time.

Teachers have little or no say over who is placed in their classes, and the curriculum they are expected to transmit is usually mandated and sometimes heavily scripted. Although teachers' classroom performances are not directly

---

CONCEPT BOX 5.2

Teachers' Roles

Teachers are classroom instructors expected to teach particular kinds and levels of curricular knowledge and skills in a fixed period of time to diverse adolescents with varying sociocultural backgrounds, abilities, and interests. They are assigned outside classroom duties, attend meetings, supervise extracurricular activities, and may also assume administrative and quasi-parenting roles.

supervised, many are indirectly monitored via their students' scores on standardized tests. Such monitoring encourages "skill-drill-kill" instructional approaches that are common to test-driven curricula (Weiner, 2006, p. 72). But teachers' approaches are much more significantly affected by the extent to which students recognize their authority.

Teachers cannot teach effectively unless students acknowledge their legitimacy as adult authority figures and are willing to comply with their orders. They must establish their dominance, which is never assured because student resistance constantly lies in wait (Pace & Hemmings, 2007). Most teachers rely on control strategies that have a significant impact on instructional methods. Among the most common are exchange, influence, and coercion (Metz, 1978). Exchange involves incentives, such as high grades or rule bending, in exchange for cooperation. Personal influence may be deployed where teachers draw on personal assets such as charm, attractiveness, or admission of vulnerabilities to win compliance (Swidler, 1979). Teachers may also resort to coercion where they reprimand, embarrass, expel, give detention to, or fail students. These kinds of control strategies do not necessarily work, and may backfire in ways that exacerbate discipline problems. Teachers lose respect if they are too lenient in their grading, too lax in rule enforcement, too buddy-buddy, too coercive, or otherwise stray too far from good instructional practice. They are treated disrespectfully by students who feel they are being disrespected by teachers who are not doing their jobs (Hemmings, 2003).

Urban public high school teachers must also contend with scarce resources, such as instructional supplies, textbooks, and classroom furnishings. There are shortages of materials in many urban schools where, for example, there may be not be enough textbooks to go around or textbooks are so damaged or outdated they are virtually useless. Other resources include support systems that provide teachers with assistance. New teachers need good mentoring, and other teachers may also require help. Far too many urban high school teachers are put into positions where they have to be resourceful without resources.

Teachers' relations with other teachers can also be challenging. It is virtually impossible for teachers to come up with well-defined classroom technologies that work in all instances with all students all of the time (Metz, 1978). Teachers generally work in isolation, which makes it difficult for them to share ideas or provide mutual support. This fact, coupled with endemic uncertainties about instructional methods causes teachers to be defensive and even hostile toward principals and colleagues who scrutinize or question what they are doing.

Certain styles of teaching nevertheless become normalized in many schools. Teachers who deviate from these styles may be sanctioned by colleagues, especially senior ones. In urban public high schools where expectations for students are low and teaching is lackadaisical, new teachers or mavericks with innovative or unusually successful approaches are often perceived as threats. Sociologically, as Payne (2008) explains, gung-ho teachers are the equivalent of factory rate-busters who are setting a pace that makes things difficult for other workers.

> If one teacher starts walking students home, parents may start asking why other teachers don't. If one teacher starts staying after school with students, the principal may think that others should, too. The rate-buster threatens settled social arrangements. (Payne, 2008, p. 22)

Some schools have instituted team teaching where groups of teachers instruct the same students, share common planning times, and otherwise work together in professional communities. This is an ideal arrangement so long as the teams are characterized by relational trust where members are mutually respectful, competent, show personal regard for one another, and have integrity (Bryk & Schneider, 2002). The problem in many urban public high schools is that many members of the teaching force may not have the attributes necessary for relational trust, or schedules do not include time for common planning.

To make matters worse, teachers are constantly subjected to a plethora of externally mandated reforms and directives without any input from them. Many have become understandably cynical about changes that, from their point of view, come and go with the whims of officials. They have no sense of ownership or personal investment in the fleeting reforms that are imposed on them.

All of these realities increase the likelihood of teacher burnout. Burnout, simply defined, involves notably negative changes in attitude and behavior in response to demanding, frustrating, and unrewarding work experiences. Among these changes are:

> loss of concern for clients and a tendency to treat clients in a detached, mechanical fashion. Other changes include increasing discouragement, pessimism, and fatalism about one's work; decline in motivation, effort, and involvement in work; apathy; negativism; frequent irritability and anger with clients and colleagues; preoccupation with one's own comfort and welfare on the job; a tendency to rationalize failure by blaming the clients of "the system"; and resistance to change, growing rigidity, and loss of creativity. (Sarason, 1996, pp. 203–204)

Burnout is an issue, but the bottom-line fact in all possibilities for urban public high schools is teachers' ultimate dependence on students.

Students

The role of students is to learn the knowledge and skills that adults deem appropriate and worthwhile for them. They are supposed to comply with official rules and codes of conduct; follow teachers' orders; do the best they can to master curriculum; and willingly subject themselves to assessments of their

CONCEPT BOX 5.3

Students' Role

The role of students is to learn knowledge and skills that adults deem worthwhile for them. They are expected to comply with rules and codes of conduct, follow teachers' orders, master curriculum, and subject themselves to assessments of their academic achievements.

academic achievement. Unlike school employees who get paid to do their jobs, students are not given monetary compensation, and in fact have little or no incentive to comply other than personal drive or adult pressure. They can play classroom ecology of games the way adult authorities want them to, or they can come up with their own playbooks.

Students are generally supportive of schooling, but they are not necessarily willing to go along with daily classroom schoolwork regimens where they have no say over task assignments with limited material rewards (Hemmings, 2003, 2004). They are required in accordance with these regimens to sign up for classes in English, social studies, the sciences, mathematics, and other subjects regardless of their personal interests. To succeed in these classes, they have to follow teachers' orders, take tests, and otherwise go along with the directions and procedures imposed on them. Schoolwork regimens are not solely about structuring academic activities. They are also about ensuring control. When teachers assign work tasks they do so with classroom management in mind. They may order students to fill out worksheets, listen quietly to lectures, and participate in other socially passive and isolating instructional routines not so much because they facilitate optimal learning, but rather because they control student behavior (McNeil, 1983, 1986).

Students may accept and even defend schoolwork regimens. But they also experience them as tedious, meaningless, difficult, time consuming, or unfair. There are times when schoolwork regimens impede rather than facilitate their progress. Students are simultaneously supportive of, and repulsed by what they are ordered to do.

Schoolwork regimens in many urban public high schools are not always or even remotely enjoyable. This fact in and of itself has a lot to do with students' willingness to comply with regimens. Compliance is also influenced by social class, ethnic, racial, and gendered sociocultural locations; socioeconomic conditions; youth culture and peer-group subcultures; and individual identity work. Students' sociocultural locations have an enormous bearing on their access to, and utilization of economic, cultural, social, and symbolic capital in educational pursuits. Such capital is taken into account in students' habitus or internalized rules of the game (Bourdieu, 1977; Bourdieu & Passeron, 1990; Brubaker, 2004; Lareau, 2001; Reed-Danahay, 2005). Habitus shapes students' thinking and behavior in relation to the educational fields (structured systems of social relations) they encounter in school.

Compliance with schoolwork regimens is also affected by socioeconomic conditions. The United States since the 1960s has undergone a momentous transformation from an industrial economic base to a postindustrial one with a demand for workers with high functional literacy, technical expertise, and other knowledge and skills distributed and certified through systems of formal education. Blue-collar jobs dried up in inner cities and drug trafficking and other illicit enterprises burgeoned. Teenagers found themselves "floating in a nebulous atmosphere" as they surveyed lawful and illicit economic opportunities and wondered whether or how to take advantage of them (Bettis, 1996, p. 115). Joblessness in inner cities made the situation much harder, especially for male adolescents from historically marginalized racial and ethnic minority groups. The decline in legitimate employment opportunities has had a devastating effect on these young men, many of whom have opted to move away from schooling and enter instead into illegal ventures to acquire money and status.

The direction taken by urban youths is profoundly influenced by youth culture and peer-group subcultures. The term *youth culture* refers to the distinctive patterns of behavior teenagers express during the transitional phase between childhood dependence and adult independence (Parsons, 1964). Many of these behaviors deviate from the dominant culture as developed by middle-class, Anglo/European sensibilities. Youth culture is widely expressed by teenagers through clothing and hair styles, slang and lingo, music, and other ways. Media feed into this culture, and merchandisers accrue huge profits from it. Youth culture is a major industry in the United States with products that are not necessarily supportive of mainstream schooling.

Adolescents form cliques and the subcultures associated with these groups are partly spinoffs of youth cultures but also draw from racial, ethnic, gender, sexual orientation, and other sociocultural sources. Subcultures are very much influenced by cliques' relationship to dominant groups, and also by how students are tracked and otherwise socially stratified in schools. They are, in other words, affected by groups' location and rank within social hierarchies. The lower the ranking, the more resistant cliques are to schooling.

Resistance is expressed through subcultural expressions in ways that reflect racial, ethnic, gender, sexual, and other affiliations and loyalties. Black student cliques, for example, may resist real and perceived White domination through oppositional cultural frames of reference and attendant expressions (Fordham, 1996; Ogbu, 1978, 1987; Ogbu & Simons, 1998). But clique subcultures do not involve clear-cut expressions of Blackness in opposition to Whiteness. Cliques produce their own particular and ever-shifting subcultural variations that may promote rather than discourage compliance with schoolwork regimens (Hemmings, 1996, 2006b).

Individual student identity work also comes into play. The cultural identity work of high school students is especially important because it provides them with a rationale for why they comply with, resist, or otherwise respond to schooling. It helps to explain why they do what they do (Staiger, 2006). Cultural identity work in urban public high schools is undertaken against the backdrop of what it means to be an educated person, which is an archetype fashioned by cultural criteria that identify people as more, or less, knowledgeable. All societies elaborate cultural practices by which particular sets of skills, knowledge, and discourses come to define what it means to be a fully educated person, and schools are the institutions where these practices are affirmed and transmitted (Levinson & Holland, 1996). High school students adopt or reject these practices as part of their identity work.

Adolescent sociocultural adaptations and identity work are thus crucial for whether urban public high school students perform their roles the way adult school authority figures would like them to. Principals, teachers, and students are the inside players on local school stages. School boards, superintendents, union officials, parents, and external partners are outside players who are ideally but not necessarily good supporting actors.

School Boards, Superintendents, Union Officials, Parents, and External Partners

School boards, superintendents, unions, parents, and external partners are not directly involved in the day-to-day operations of urban public high schools, but they nevertheless wield significant influence over schooling. School boards are elected bodies entrusted with lay oversight of K-12 public schools. Members are responsible for setting the overall district vision for education and attendant policies. They establish short- and long-term goals; review school performance indicators and student assessments; plan and approve district budgets; negotiate contracts with labor unions; oversee service contracts and facilities maintenance; and generate revenue through capital campaigns, bonds, tax levies, and other means (Danzberger, Kirst, & Usdan, 1992, 1993; Land, 2002; Resnick, 1999). School boards also hire superintendents to handle the administration of district schools.

Superintendents are essentially chief executive officers (Hoyle, Bjork, Collier, & Glass, 2005; Kowalski, 2005; Land, 2002). They work with school boards on the development, implementation, and evaluation of policies, programs, and services. They oversee processes for recruiting, selecting, and assigning employees, and for grievance and dismissal procedures. They ensure fiscal soundness in day-to-day operations and prepare recommendations for annual budgets and tax rates. Superintendents also play a crucial role in district-wide communication systems especially communications with the community. And they are supposed to promote student academic achievement.

Teacher unions negotiate and ensure the enforcement of contracts with school districts that include agreements pertaining to monetary compensation, benefits, and pay scales for teachers; processes for hiring, dismissing, and transferring teachers; grievance procedures; and clauses regarding professional development, working conditions, and other instructional support. Many also work with school boards on reform initiatives.

The relationship between parents and schools is a two-way street. School actors cannot play their parts in the schooling process unless parents play supportive roles. Parents support their children by instilling a work ethic, making sure homework is completed, insisting on respect for teachers, and through other means. They support teachers by taking responsibility for building relationships with them and putting "praise before blame" wherever they can (Fullan, 2007, p. 205). It is also very important for parents to uphold the authority of good teachers. Their relationships with teachers are vital and ideally reciprocal and mutually respectful.

Interinstitutional collaborations with urban public high schools that involve institutions of higher education, corporations, industries, community agencies, and other external partners are common, and some argue, necessary for true reform (Zimpher & Howey, 2004). External partners can help schools create or expand their social capital through footholds in networks with access to valuable resources. They can assist with educational initiatives through the expertise of their employees or utilization of their facilities and equipment. Most partnerships emerge organically and are usually characterized by pressures to move fast. They are commonly cohort partnerships created for a specific project or task, conceived and launched outside of schools, and funded by grants (Sirotnik & Goodlad, 1988). When the project is completed, or funding ends, the partnership dissolves. Results are often temporary or locked in time (Slater, 1996).

How school boards, superintendents, unions, parents, and external partners play their roles should support the role performances of effective principals, teachers, and students. But this is not what happens in the local staging areas of many urban public high schools. The power of urban school boards to accommodate public high schools has greatly diminished over the years because of escalating federal and state controls. The federal government in the 1950s began to assume greater control over public school districts through legislated programs with provisions for federal funding. Federally funded Title I, bilingual education, and other programs continued to proliferate in the 1960s and 1970s, and states since the 1980s have also asserted more control over schools. States have issued stricter requirements for standardized curriculum and testing, teacher certification, graduation standards, and data collection (Carol et al. 1986; Danzberger, Carol, et al., 1987; Danzberger, Kirst, & Usdan, 1992; Resnick, 1999; Rothman, 1992). The No Child Left Behind Act of 2001 expanded federal control over

public education much further and more deeply. Such incursions have significantly undermined the authority of school boards to the point where there are
debates over whether they should remain (Land, 2002).

The situation in many urban districts is worsened by school board members
having a very difficult time working together as a cohesive group. Members
are under the influence of special interest groups, political ideologies, strong
personalities, or other divisive forces (Anderson, 1992).

Urban school boards have also been criticized for their inability to collaborate effectively with superintendents (Carol et al. 1986; Danzberger, 1992,
1994; Goodman & Zimmerman, 2000; Land, 2002). There has been a revolv-

---

CONCEPT BOX 5.4

**Roles of School Boards, Superintendents,
Unions, Parents, and External Partners**

School Boards: Set overall vision and policies; establish short- and long-
term goals; review school performance and student assessments; plan
and approve district budgets; negotiate contracts with unions; oversee
service contracts and facilities maintenance; generate revenue; and
hire and oversee superintendents.

Superintendents: Chief executive officers who work with school boards
on the development, implementation, and evaluation of policies,
programs, and services. They are involved in employee recruitment,
selection, and assignment; grievance and dismissal procedures; fiscal
aspects of daily operations; recommendations for annual budgets and
tax rates; district-wide communication systems; and promotion of student academic achievement.

Teacher Unions: Negotiate and ensure the enforcement of contracts with
school districts with agreements pertaining to monetary compensation, benefits, and pay scales for teachers; processes for hiring, dismissing, and transferring teachers; grievance procedures; and clauses
regarding professional development, working conditions, and other
instructional support. They may also work with school boards on
reform initiatives.

Parents: Support their children by instilling a work ethic, making sure
homework is completed, insisting on respect for teachers, and other
means. They support teachers by building relationships with them,
putting "praise before blame," and uphold their authority.

External Partners: Create or expand the social capital of schools through
networks with access to valuable resources; assist with educational initiatives through the expertise of their employees or utilization of their
facilities and equipment.

ing door of superintendents in urban public school districts partly as a result of discord within and with school boards. The shelf life of superintendents is not always related to the quality of their work. Superintendents may actually reduce the number of failing schools, raise test scores, rebuild dilapidated faculties, or institute other substantial improvements. But unremitting friction between them and school boards and also with teachers unions can, and does, drive them off (Payne, 2008).

Teacher unions in urban school districts are notorious for their seemingly self-interested efforts to negotiate lucrative contracts for their members. Through contracts negotiated under the threat of strikes or other disruptive actions, unions have managed to circumscribe the power of building principals, and given teachers, especially senior faculty, substantial authority over the schools, grade levels, and tracks to which they are assigned (Payne, 2008). They have in many situations generated animosity and conflict rather than mutually beneficial or reform-minded collaboration.

Parents' interest in and knowledge of their own children's learning is generally not capitalized on in urban public high schools. There is asymmetrical power, and low-income parents are especially "vulnerable and unconfident" in their relationships with schools, especially if teachers make little or no effort to connect with them (Fullan, 2007, p. 193). Parents are distrustful, leery of making contact with their child's school, and when they do make contact they feel they are not being heard. Many teachers exacerbate the situation by placing the blame for students' poor performance squarely on the shoulders of parents. They point the finger at parental substance abuse, unemployment, lack of interest in education, and otherwise play the blame games promoted in provincial versions of deficit theories. Distrust begets distrust which never bodes well for parent–teacher relations.

Interinstitutional initiatives that involve urban public high schools working in collaboration with institutions of higher education, corporations, industries, community agencies, and other external partners are important. But they often falter due to lack of planning, mistrust, differences between organizational cultures, dissimilar goals, and poor communication (Center for Higher Educational Policy Analysis, 2005). The people involved in these initiatives behave in accordance with the sociopolitical logics of their own organizational cultures transmitted through messages about their identity, status, and power within the system (Slater, 1996). These messages are translated by individuals into beliefs about what is or ought to be possible through the roles they play and exchanges they make. Pernicious politics are incited between and within partnering organizations when people work at all cost to maintain who they are, secure high status, or be in control.

Relationships are the most fundamental element in how inside and external school actors perform their roles. Relationships are the crux of school dramas that can be positively uplifting or destructively tragic.

School Dramas

Much scholarship on urban public high schools is quantitatively oriented and relies on research methods conducive for gathering and analyzing statistical data. A much less utilized but quite revealing research approach is school ethnography where researchers spend a prolonged period of time in schools doing fieldwork that entails extended observations, in-depth interviews with school actors, and the gathering of archival data. Ethnography and qualitative research spinoffs illuminate life in offices, classrooms, and corridors in ways that are impossible with quantitative research. The data this research generate are used to create thick descriptions of how school actors actually perform their roles in relation to one another within the constraints and freedoms of internal school cultures and structures, and in response to external directives. They "culminate in a 'picture' containing diverse details ordinarily not studied in relation to each other" and reveal the stark realities of how difficult and challenging schooling can be in local school staging areas (Sarason, 1996, p. 176). Ethnographic and qualitative research uncovers and elucidates everyday school dramas.

What ethnographic and qualitative research has revealed is how demoralized and dysfunctional urban public high schools are (Davidson, 1996; Garot, 2010; Hemmings, 2000a, 2002, 2003, 2004); Michie, 1999; Payne, 2008; Staiger, 2006; Valenzuela, 1999). These schools are staging areas for tragic dramas in classrooms and corridors, and are an awful and often unsolvable problem for the principals who have to deal with them.

Classroom Dramas

The ideal for teachers in their role performances is to enact publicly endorsed instructional scripts. There are basic common scripts for "The American High School" for scheduling, curricular content, assessment, and the practical realization of other ritual classifications. Teachers are expected to adhere to these scripts and also to classroom screenplays for the "educated person" in keeping with the cultural practices and particular sets of skills, knowledge, and discourses associated with dominant notions of what it means to be fully educated (Levinson & Holland, 1996, p. 2). To be fully educated is to embrace and utilize middle-class, Anglo/European American values, language, beliefs, and norms as well as mainstream academic knowledge and skills.

Despite the widespread endorsement of common scripts for schooling, teachers in many urban public high schools deviate from them in response to the daily dramas that unfold in their classrooms. Many of them end up engaging in defensive teaching where they water down curriculum, assign meaningless seatwork, and otherwise defend themselves through simplified and educationally feeble instructional scripting (McNeil, 1983). Patterns of defensive teaching were common in my own observations of urban high school classrooms (Hemmings, 2003, 2004, 2006a). Teachers felt enormous pressure to follow common scripts that would promote student achievement, but they were constantly stymied by highly social and disaffected students, externally imposed directives, lack of support and resources, little or no interaction with other teachers, and other instructionally crippling forces. I watched students in classroom after classroom talking, yelling, laughing loudly, sleeping, passing notes, swearing, eating, hugging, hitting, and otherwise playing around within their own ecology of games. I saw teachers agonizing over their lack of authority and uncertainties about how to instruct and discipline their students. The vast majority would pass out worksheets or ask students to write out answers to textbook questions, and then sit down at their desks, wander quietly around the room, or otherwise fade into the background.

Garot (2010) describes this pattern at its worst in his ethnographic study of an alternative urban public high school where most students were low-income Blacks and Latinos and some were members of street gangs. He describes the prevailing instructional approach that teachers adopted as an educationally crushing "pedagogy of oppression."

> By and large, students … [did] one of two things: either complete questions on a worksheet or answer questions at the end of a chapter in a book. Directed lessons [were] rare because of problems with absenteeism, but when teachers [did] provide substantive lectures these [were] often quite misinformative. More commonly, teachers gave "life experience" lectures in hopes of edifying students by sharing practical wisdom. (pp. 24–25)

Substitute teachers were a common classroom presence because teachers were constantly calling in sick. One classroom scene involving a substitute teacher provides a vivid description of how oppressive life in classrooms could be.

> A substitute teacher sat at the teacher's desk. The students looked to be in pain, frustrated, and miserable, but still with their somewhat rebellious senses of humor. Sean was talking to himself at the front table when I entered. I sat down next to Tom and looked into his bloodshot eyes. He had a ragtag dictionary in front of him and [was] aimlessly flipped through pages. "Man, this sucks," he told me. He said all they had to do was look up sixteen words and write sentences with them. Antione had actually done it, and the sub graded it, noticing that one sentence was missing a period and emphasizing to Antione how important that was. Antione took the paper with a limp hand that fell with the paper. I pointed out to Tom that all the words started with a "p." "That don't mean nothin'," he said. "She just picks out any words. Today, they just happen to begin with 'p.' "Oh," I said. (Garot, 2010, p. 26)

Relations between teachers and students revolve around issues of power and authority. During my fieldwork in urban high schools I observed first-hand how students would challenge their teachers' authority. It became apparent in many classrooms that many students were acting out in defense of school regimens. They were especially hard on teachers who entirely abdicated their instructional roles or treated them with obvious disrespect. Students would put pressure on despicably disrespectful teachers to assume positions of authority that were worthy of respect.

An example is an AP psychology teacher I observed at a desegregated urban high school (Hemmings, 2003, p. 425). The teacher, Mr. Harrison, was a White man in his late 40s. He taught in an irreverent manner that had no direct connection to the AP curriculum. He would devote most of the class period to off-color discussions focusing on sex, sexuality, and what he called "theories of love." He asked students on one occasion what they thought "intimate" meant. A White boy answered, "It's smooching without fondling." Another boy said it was "cuddling, kissing, and light petting on top of pants instead of inside them." Mr. Harrison said in a serious voice, "Yes, yes that's a good way to feel it out."

Some of the students in the class were clearly outraged. A girl cried out that he was "a disgrace to his profession and offensive as hell." A boy demanded that he "cut the crap." Another girl told me after class that "horny Harrison's class is over before it starts and we're the ones who are getting screwed." When I asked Mr. Harrison to explain his teaching style, he told me with a wry smile that his intent was to "stimulate the real interests of kids."

Most urban public high school teachers are not as blatantly cynical or contemptuous as Mr. Harrison. But a number of them do experience difficulties in establishing their authority over students who are ever-poised to challenge teachers who are incompetent, disengaged, disrespectful, or are way out of line with what they think schooling ought to be. Much of their resistance is actually about the upholding of common scripts for schooling. It is also affected by corridor dramas.

Corridor Dramas

High school students spend about an hour during the school day in hallways, lunchrooms, bathrooms, and other corridor spaces. Forty-five minutes of this time is typically allocated for passage between classes (5 minutes between periods) and for lunch (20 minutes). Students also gather for about 15 minutes before and after school. This hour, less than 1/6th of the official schedule, belongs to students and is the time when they engage in social dramas with profound consequences.

Corridor dramas run the gamut from playful adolescent sociability to interpersonally destructive hostility. My initial impression of corridor life in the urban high schools I studied was that it was chaotic (Hemmings, 2000, 2004). Hallways were packed with teenagers leaning against lockers or walls conversing with their friends, walking in pairs or packs, holding each other in lover embraces, or delivering fleeting punches and verbal insults. Social patterns emerged over time and it became apparent that students divided themselves into cliques along racial, ethnic, and gender lines. Cliques in my research sites had names and symbolic markers that conveyed who members were and what they stood for. There were "skinheads," "head bangers," and "grunge." Skinheads were White working-class boys who shaved their heads, tattooed swastikas on their arms, and otherwise emulated extremist neo-Nazi hate groups. Head bangers mimicked rogue motorcycle gangs with their shiny black leather jackets draped in chains. Grunge looked like prison inmates with their oversized jeans that sagged and drooped low in the behind. Teenagers across these groups pierced small gold rings through their ears, noses, lips, eyebrows and, I was told, genitals.

Some of the Black male students were known as "playas" (players) and their female counterparts were "fly girls" or "hoochies." Other Black students wore sports-team or name-brand overcoats throughout the day or preferred designer clothes which carried Tommy Hilfiger, Nautica, Versace, and other expensive manufacturing labels.

There were real and pseudo street gangs. One was an all-White gang known as Gangsters with Drama or "GWD." Another was a racially mixed gang called "PHP" or Prentice Heights Posse. Each displayed special colors, insignia, and other signs of their affiliations. There also was an artistic group of kids who looked and acted like 1960s hippies. Known as the JHUBWT (Jefferson High Underwater Basket Weaving Team), they wore tie-dyed shirts and bell-bottomed jeans and smoked marijuana. There were "normal kids" who wore regular blue jeans, moderately priced athletic shoes, t-shirts, sweatshirts, and other neutral apparel. Some students were identified as high achievers—"geeks," "nerds," and "brainiacs"—who everyone agreed were a distinct minority.

In other more multiracial and multiethnic urban schools, race and ethnicity are very important factors in corridor politics. In an ethnographic study of Roosevelt High, an urban high school in California, Staiger (2006) found that African American, Cambodian, Latino, Samoan, and White Anglo/European American peer groups were competing and occasionally fighting with one another for dominance. Blacks were at the top and Cambodians forged symbolic alliances with them. Latinos gravitated toward White Anglo/European American students, and Samoans stood by as respected peacemakers. Another group of students in an upper-track program identified themselves as gay. They projected an image of sexual nonconformity and, as Staiger (2006) explains, worked it on several fronts to set themselves apart from "proper, preppy and conservative students" and to "draw a clear line between [themselves and] the outwardly macho posture of [Black males] and what they considered the dominant Black masculinity on campus" (p. 162).

I heard several stories from students in my own research about how they or others had money and goods stolen, conned, or beaten out of them. A White student told me that his locker had been broken into so many times that he no longer used it. I heard a gut-wrenching tale about a Black student who had been robbed twice at knifepoint. He had been an outgoing person and a good student with college aspirations. After the second robbery, he became despondent, was often absent from school, and eventually dropped out.

Bullying and victimization were common. Fistfights were less frequent yet exciting performances that usually began with a challenger yelling obscenities at the person he or she wanted to fight. The yelling of obscenities was the public announcement for students to gather as an audience. Combatants would commence the fight when the audience was assembled. Much was at stake in these performances as winners won respect and status and losers lost standing in relation to their peers. Gaining respect was imperative for garnering power to assert, challenge, or ward off control in interactions with other students. To lose respect was to become powerless, subordinate, and vulnerable to abuse (Gordon, 1997). Fights under such circumstances could be fierce and sometimes injurious to the point where students were hospitalized. They usually ended with the arrival of security guards who separated combatants and ceremoniously escorted them to the principal's office.

There were also dramas around gendered antagonisms. Girls were often subjected to male sexual harassment. Boys would hit or grope them and call them "hoes" (whores), "bitches," or "White ass." Many girls fought back by positioning themselves as docile and not-so-docile female bodies (Adams, 1999). They would act like "nice" girls in an effort to get disrespectful boys to treat them more respectfully. But they also projected images as tough girls with reputations for being just as capable as boys of winning respect through physical strength, aggression, and fearless counterattacks. Some girls would physically retaliate when boys harassed them. A Black girl told me about how she handled boys who touched her in the hallways. "I tell them to get their fucking hands off me." A White girl told me about a boy who kept fondling her in a class. The teacher would not stop it and she finally lost her temper and "kicked the jerk in the face." The fondling ended. Girls also fought with other girls, especially those who moved in on their boyfriends or otherwise showed disrespect for them and their relationships.

These kinds of corridor dramas were usually fleeting and often went unnoticed by adults. Students had to find their own strategies to deal with them if they wanted to survive or stay in school. Teachers were generally aware of what was happening in corridors, but most stayed out of student frays. They left it up to principals who, especially in the case of fights and dangerous acts of violence involving weaponry, would expel students, issue in-school suspensions, or call the police. Principals were not only expected to deal with classroom and corridor dramas, but also with external directives that often did not make their jobs any easier.

Principal Dramas

Ideally urban high school principals are visible leaders with inspiring educational visions who can effectively promote high student achievement, maintain orderly school environments, and establish good working relations with teacher unions, district officials, and external partners. Enormous pressure has been placed on them in recent years to be reform-minded leaders capable of generating positive change.

The reality for many principals is quite different and anything but ideal. They are overwhelmed by what a principal described to me as "functionalities"—daily incidents that have a direct bearing on how schools actually function. She wrote the following account of "A Day of My Life:"

> 6:15 Arrived at school, responded to email and attempted unsuccessfully to organize my desk enough to get those documents I most needed in front of me. There were 432 emails remaining in my inbox (I purge regularly, but get about 80 a day). For yesterday, the new ones included:
>
> 14 directives from central office—one from the treasurer's office asking if we knew anything about a certain teacher, or if she had ever taught there. Yes, I replied, she teaches here every day and is on the HR rosters for my school and your department sends her a paycheck every two weeks. OK, I was more diplomatic than that, but it does make you wonder whether or when the central office support mechanisms ever talk to each other.
>
> 17 requests for meetings
>
> 6 invitations to participate in an interview, discussion, webinar, PD, or brain-pick of one sort or another. Some of these look really interesting, but you can't do most of them.
>
> 3 press contacts
>
> 3 requests to fill out surveys
>
> 9 questions from staff members on issues in progress
>
> 8 regarding special ed matters
>
> 9 on specific discipline matters
>
> 3 from the legal department
>
> 2 from the state
>
> 6 from private interests
>
> 11 on calendar events including sports events
>
> Of course, I hardly made a dent in these, just skimmed, answered those most critical so that certain problems didn't become bottlenecked waiting for some indication of direction from me. Deleted all that I could without consequence.
>
> 7:30 Parent conference regarding a suspension of a girl who produces regular confrontations and sometimes fights with her peers. One part consequences. One part counseling. One part warning.

8:00 Walked up the street (2 blocks) to a local carryout where our kids congregate in the mornings resulting in underage tobacco sales. Older kids trying to gang recruit and fight our boys or make sexual contact with our girls.

8:20 Supervision in North Cafeteria. We have a thousand kids and two lunchrooms, with a total capacity of 650. Getting kids to move in, stand around, get breakfast, stay cool.

8:35 Hall supervision in Bridge area. Spoke with 3 parents arriving for conferences. Made a dozen freshmen kids tuck in their uniform shirts, and asked a senior boy to pull up his panties, as his jeans were dangling around his knees.

8:45 Supervision in stairwell G to make sure late kids go past the tardy center.

8:55 Met w/ two secretaries to review drafts of newsletter. Drafted note to parents in the newsletter about the carryout problem in the morning.

OK, now losing all track of time. Took a phone call from legal, conducted a random search with the district's security response team, investigated a stairwell sex incident, a stolen master key incident, and met with a distraught instructional aide following a break-in and theft in her classroom. Hmm, yes, that turned out to be related to the stolen master key. Admonished a late teacher, spoke with a student about her asthma, sent a teacher out for an observation schedule, conducted a search for contraband in the ceiling of a classroom, called another principal for an observation request, stopped in to say hello to a tutoring resource, a corporate rep, and two staff members, referred three teachers to local university administration prep program, talked to Facilities about a construction problem in the $40 million renovation project. Processed 6 disciplinary referrals, meeting with the students and calling all their parents, referred 8 more to their program facilitators, stopped by the Blackboard tech training, met with a department chair, met with the secretary on scheduling, met w/ the AP to catch up on 2 discipline cases, an IEP case, and a teacher evaluation case, wrote a bunch of memos and updates. Ran out for a 2:00 meeting at the central office, back at 3:00 for a construction walk-through with the project manager, construction manager, and district facilities manager, our tech teacher, and our staffer who's responsible for developing our demo lab in a space where all the wrong stuff was installed. Met some teachers at a local watering hole to deliver the beverage I had promised. Ran to a local coffee shop to order breakfast stuff for our staff writing/research group the next morning. Took a call from my mentee processing her day and a decision she had to make. Ran to dinner with a friend, ran into a teacher at the restaurant and wished I had more of a chance to socialize with my staff, who are very interesting and fun people, stopped back by the coffee shop (It's now about 9:15 p.m.), went home, built a fire, checked the sub lists for the next day, called 2 subs, and checked messages.

Her typical days are frenetic, shifting rapidly from one incident to the next involving rapid-fire decisions in response to an astronomical number of e-mail messages; student thefts, break-ins, inappropriate sexual behavior, disciplinary referrals, and other infractions; facilities; parent conferences; lunchroom supervision; and a host of other issues, problems, and events requiring immediate attention. Rather than be proactive leaders, she and many other urban high school principals are reactive because of the constant bombardment of daily demands that occupy their attention sometimes well into the night.

Principals must also respond to federal, state, and district office directives, teacher unions, and external partners. These outside entities have their own agendas that may not be in sync with what principals think is best for their schools, and that, more often than not, are not sensitive to the daily realities of life in schools serving large numbers of working-class and low-income youths of color. Another urban high school principal who was noted for his exceptionally effective leadership told me that a "good day was one where we didn't have to deal with something from the district office" or other external pressures. He and other principals had enough to contend with regarding the internal dramas in the local staging areas of their schools. Having to deal with the political and other dramas of outsiders did not necessarily help their causes much less the realization of sustainable reform possibilities. Urban public high school dramas are thus more tragic than hopeful.

Summation

Historical, sociological, anthropological, and political foundations of education are critical for explaining the current state of urban public high schools and providing vital insights for future possibilities. They set the stage for understanding high schools as local staging areas where school actors perform their roles in the midst of crushing pressures that adversely affect everyday school dramas.

Internal school actors, principals, teachers, and students, are expected to perform their roles in particular ways. School boards, teacher unions, superintendents, parents, organizational partners, and other external actors all have important support roles to play. If these actors are able to perform their roles in ideal ways, then schooling works for all concerned. When they cannot, then schools deteriorate into demoralizing conditions characterized by disabling organizational cultures and dysfunctional structures. Unfortunately, school actors in many urban public high schools are unable to perform their expected roles because they are overpowered by a multitude of daunting demands, scarcity of resources, obtrusive directives, internal and external politics, student resistance, teacher burnout, principal overload, and larger societal, cultural, and economic realities.

How urban public high school teachers, students, and principals ultimately play their roles in relation to one another constitute the actual plots of everyday life in classrooms, corridors, and administrative offices. Teachers in classroom dramas often end up engaging in defensive teaching where they water down curriculum, assign meaningless seatwork, and otherwise defend themselves. Students during the time they spend in corridor spaces divide themselves into distinctive cliques usually along racial, ethnic, and gendered lines. They express their identities, solidify groups, compete for dominance, and defend themselves through fistfight performances, flashy attire, oral assertions, and other dramatic presentations. Principals in their daily and nightly dramas engage in rapid-fire decision making in reaction to countless messages, problems, issues, and directives. They are the ones who are supposed to direct the school play. But instead of guiding the production to endings that everyone can applaud, many of them are stymied or utterly defeated by the sheer tragedy of the situation they and other school actors find themselves in. They are in desperate need of change that will help them to produce more positive, less destructive school plots.

Local School Staging Areas

Discussion Questions

1. Principals, teachers, students, school board members, union officials, superintendents, parents, and external partners are the school actors most responsible for making sure that students are provided with good schooling. Why is it so difficult for them to collaborate in urban public high school settings?
2. Urban high school principals have a difficult time carrying out their roles as instructional leaders. They do not feel they are in a position to improve ineffective teaching. Why do they feel this way and what if anything can be done about it?
3. Many teachers in urban public high schools engage in defensive teaching that Garot (2010) describes as an educationally crushing "pedagogy of oppression." Why do they resort to this approach, and are there ways to implement more empowering pedagogies in troubled urban public high schools?
4. Urban public high school student corridor dramas run the gamut from playful adolescent sociability to destructive hostility. How can or should corridor violence, harassment, and other injurious behavior be mediated?
5. External school actors can enhance or undermine effective schooling. How might they better serve or support internal school actors?

6

URBAN PUBLIC HIGH SCHOOL REFORM

Fundamental Facts of Schooling

Constructive discussions of real and sustainable possibilities for urban public high school reform rely on practical understandings of the fundamental facts of schooling. These facts, described and explicated below, pertain to:

- Classroom dynamics
- School organizational cultures, structures, and moral orders
- Principal leadership
- Local community characteristics
- Federal, state, and district educational directives
- Multi-institutional partnerships

Classroom Dynamics

The bottom line and most important fact of schooling is *classroom dynamics*. The success of all reforms ultimately depends on teachers and students and the classroom regimens and relations they produce. To be effective in urban classrooms, teachers need relevant credentials, ongoing professional development, a command of pedagogical content knowledge, practical experience, and other qualifications that enable them to instruct, assess, and direct the conduct of racially, ethnically, and economically diverse students. The most qualified teachers possess credentials from accredited teacher education programs that actually prepare them for the challenges of urban public schooling. They participate in suitable and contextualized professional development. And they have a command of pedagogical content knowledge where they not only have a strong mastery of subject matter content, but also a repertoire of pedagogical techniques for representing and formulating content in ways that make it

---

CONCEPT BOX 6.1

Fundamental Facts of Schooling

1. *Classroom Dynamics:* Schooling ultimately depends on teachers and students and the classroom regimens and relations they produce.
2. *School Organizational Culture, Structures, and Moral Orders:* Classroom dynamics are affected by school organizational cultures that are socially constructed within semibureaucratic structures. Moral orders convey meanings about what is right and wrong for curriculum, leadership, pedagogy, behavior, and character.
3. *Principal Leadership:* Principals play pivotal roles in the production and maintenance of school cultures, structures, and moral orders that support instruction, learning, order, and relations.
4. *Local Community Characteristics:* Urban communities and neighborhoods are characterized by social, cultural, and economic conditions that affect school/community relations and students' commitment to formal schooling.
5. *Federal, State, and District Directives:* Directives are formulated and imposed as top-down policies, regulations, legislation, court orders, and programs that do not necessarily address the realities of school operations. They generally do not hold originators accountable for their results.
6. *Multi-Institutional Partnerships:* Partnerships emerge organically and are good avenues for distributing social capital, sharing and pooling resources, improving delivery of services, and strengthening school/community relations. Partners may share a common interest in improving schools, but each operates in accordance with their own organizational cultures, goals, interests, and logics of sociopolitical relations.

---

effectively teachable to urban youths (Shulman, 2000). The practice of assigning the least experienced teachers to the most challenging students should end. Students in urban public high schools deserve, and absolutely must have the most qualified teachers.

Classroom dynamics also revolve around the fact that the regularities of teaching and learning are structured by schoolwork regimens, which are comprised of instructional delivery methods (e.g., lectures, recitations, small-group work, projects, etc.), assignments, tests, disciplinary procedures, and other routines that students may accept in principle but resist in practice. Optimal regimens engage students in real learning, maintain order, and promote academic achievement. Ineffective ones are those where teachers are constantly defending themselves through overly simplified instruction and lax discipline to the point where students experience them as tedious, meaningless, and downright insulting.

Classroom dynamics ultimately depend on teacher–student relations, the decisive determinant of whether or how effective regimens are produced. Teachers and students during the course of their relations construct what life in classrooms is actually like. Their relations are profoundly affected by who is granted authority and how authority is exercised. Teachers, simply put, cannot engineer effective regimens and win student compliance unless they have the authority to do so. Their authority is greatly undermined when policymakers, politicians, and legislators publicly criticize them in the media. It is destroyed when students do not respect them or they do not respect students. Public and mutual respect is thus crucial in classroom dynamics.

School Organizational Cultures, Structures, and Moral Orders

Another fundamental fact of schooling is *school organizational cultures, structures, and moral orders*. Classrooms are embedded in, and directly affected by, school organizational cultures that are socially constructed within semibureaucratic organizational structures. School cultures are comprised of understandings that in the most ideal conditions bind school actors to each other and to their school. Such cultures are characterized by outward expressions, behavioral norms, and deeply held values that are most conducive for educational success. Prevailing school organizational cultures have a profound impact on overall administrative and faculty operations as well as administrator, teacher, staff, and student subcultures. They are disabling for the school as a whole and individuals in particular if they are characterized by disrespect and distrust, self-serving politics, lackadaisical work norms, and conflicting values.

Conceptually, school organizational structure refers to formal roles and responsibilities, modes of supervision, technologies related to work processes, scheduling, governance, and other systems set up to fulfill formal goals (Weber, 1925/1947). As noted in earlier chapters, schools are semibureaucratic structures with tightly coupled ritualized systems of classification (e.g., credentialing, class schedules, curricular topics, guidelines, and graduation requirements) and loosely coupled activity structures where administrators and teachers have some autonomy (Metz, 1978; Weick, 1983). High schools have tracking structures where students are sorted into different classes with differentiated curriculum. Schools also have governance structures that run the gamut from top-down decision making where principals rule the roost to more democratic arrangements that rely on teacher leadership and shared decision making. Functional structures are those where systems operate in ways that lead to the fulfillment of educational goals. Systems in dysfunctional structures are broken and contribute to the institutionalization of failure.

Moral orders are notable parts of school organizational cultures and have a direct bearing on whether or how structural systems function. The understandings that constitute these orders carry moral overtones of right and wrong that color the meanings of worthwhile curriculum, proper pedagogy, and good character in ways that have a profound impact on what should or ought to happen in administrative offices, classrooms, and corridors (Hemmings, 2006a). Good moral orders are permeated with sound morality and educational ethics that are shared and enacted by school actors. Orders are demoralizing when they are riddled with conflicting, counterproductive, and unethical understandings about what should happen in offices, classrooms, and corridors.

Smoothly operating urban public high schools have organizational rationality sustained by positive school cultures, well-functioning structures, and good moral orders. Rationality exists when organizational ends are practically aligned with appropriate means. Schools become irrational when they are marred by disabling organizational cultures, dysfunctional structures, and demoralized administrators, teachers, and students. School actors in such environments become invested in failure rather than success because it releases them from accountability, encourages them to cut the best deals for themselves, and frees them to "generally blow off the least pleasant aspects of their jobs" (Payne, 2008, p. 60). It becomes a situation of each man, woman, and teenager for him- or herself.

Principal Leadership

School principal leadership is a determinant fact of schooling. Principals are pinnacle leaders who play pivotal roles in the production and maintenance of school cultures, structures, and moral orders that support good instruction, genuine learning, orderly environments, and good working relationships. Their job is to bring school actors together in the construction and realization of a shared educational vision driven by a sense of moral purpose (Deal & Peterson, 1990; Fullan & Hargreaves, 1992; Senge, 1990). The most effective principals understand that good leadership is contextualized. They set internal processes in motion that enable school actors to progressively learn how to do what they need to do to achieve goals. Elmore (2000) refers to this as organized social learning where leaders intentionally mobilize the collective capacity of school actors to figure out how to teach and learn within the circumstances they find themselves in. To be successful in urban public high schools, principals need to know how systems and individuals interact in the day-to-day, nitty-gritty of school life, and how to foster mutual respect, trust, on-the-job learning, flexibility, risk-taking, innovation, and adaptation to change (Fullan, 2007; Fullan & Hargreaves, 1992). They must be able to recruit and retain strong teachers, and dismiss incompetent and weak ones. They empower the best teachers through the institutionalization of professional community teams, common planning times, and other ways for teachers to meet, plan, and govern together on a regular basis. And they interact with, and get to know, students in their school. Ineffective principals are overwhelmed by daily demands and events, do not include teachers in decision making, are virtually invisible, and have no sense of how cultures and structures affect teaching and learning.

Local Community Characteristics

An understanding of *local community characteristics* is fundamental to a comprehension of urban high schools. These schools serve communities that vary significantly in terms of racial, ethnic, and social class demographics and socioeconomic opportunities for adults and young people, and these issues directly affect students' faith in and capacity to take advantage of formal schooling.

Many urban public high schools serve neighborhoods where racial, immigrant, and ethnic minority groups reside. As noted in earlier chapters, schools in the United States have a long tradition of Americanization through the transmission of curriculum steeped in Anglo/European American academic content and cultural meanings. Students' natal home cultures with their particular styles of learning, communication, and literacy may be quite different from cultural expectations endorsed in schools. Misunderstandings caused by home–school cultural discontinuities can lead to conflict and ultimately to school failure if students and teachers are unable to make responsive cultural adaptations (Erickson, 1987; Phelan, Davidson, & Yu, 1993, 1998). Conflict may be especially acute for Black students, Chicanos, Latinos, and youths from other racial and ethnic groups that have been subjected to historical subordination, exploitation, and discrimination by the dominant White majority (Ogbu, 1978, 1987; Ogbu & Simons, 1998). Racial and ethnic minority students may resist schooling as part of their cultural identity work and to stay socially connected to their communities.

Poverty also has a profound impact on school–community relations. Chronic joblessness in impoverished urban neighborhoods has had socially destructive consequences for residents (Wilson, 1996). Teenagers and young adults, especially young men, are foregoing formal education and resorting to drug trafficking and other illicit means to acquire money, status, and power. This has led to exorbitantly high assault and murder rates. When violence is a regular part of neighborhood life it spills over into schools where security guards, metal detectors, shakedowns, frequent searches for weapons and contraband, and calls to the police are far too common.

The effectiveness of schools depends on the relationships school actors forge with parents, community leaders, social services, and agencies. Principals, teachers, and support staff must find ways to work with rather than against the communities they serve. They need to make a concerted effort to address the social, cultural, and emotional issues that students bring with them to school. Social and emotional learning skills related to conflict resolution, managing emotions under stress, and affirming and accommodating cultural differences should be conveyed and reinforced. Fights for respect and dominance have to be mediated, and other strategies for strengthening relations and resolving hostilities should be attempted. Ineffective schools are inevitably those where school–community relations have deteriorated to the point where school violence, student resistance to learning, parent and community anger and alienation, and teacher fear and frustration are pervasive.

Federal, State, and District Educational Directives

Possibilities for reform are also affected by *federal, state, and district educational directives,* which are usually formulated and imposed as top-down policies, regulations, legislation, court orders, and programs. The fundamental fact of the matter is that these directives can significantly undermine rather than enhance effective schooling, and generally do not hold the people who issue them accountable for their results or impact on schools. Directives are often more politically driven and ideologically laden than practically conceived or honed with school realities in mind. Those that take into account classroom dynamics, school cultures and structures, the pivotal leadership of school principals, and local community characteristics are more likely to contribute in positive ways to urban public high school improvement and reform. Directives that ignore the realities of urban schooling can cause enormous harm.

Historically, the most destructive directives were those that were hurried or imposed with little or no sensitivity to school operations. Court ordered desegregation in the 1970s unsettled cohesive school cultures and led to the mass flight of middle-class families from urban public schools (Orfield, Eaton, & the Harvard Project on School Desegregation, 1996). In recent years, No Child Left Behind and other accountability legislation has created incentives for teachers to "teach to the test" through "skill-drill-kill" instructional approaches (Weiner, 2006), and for schools to devote less time to science, social studies, history, geography, foreign languages, art, and music (Ravitch, 2010). It has stigmatized and shut down many multiracial, multiethnic, and high-poverty urban public high schools. Such legislation has made things much worse for many students who had attended these schools, who are already among the most likely to be subjected to low expectations and dumbed-down instruction.

Federal, state, and district directives most conducive for effective schooling are those that involve principals, teachers, and other school actors in their conception and implementation. They hold everyone accountable for their results not just the people expected to follow them.

Multi-Institutional Partnerships

Multi-institutional partnerships are multiplying and may be instrumental in improving urban public high schools. They are more likely to emerge organically rather than by being imposed on schools in a directive fashion, and are much more conducive for democratic collaboration. Partnerships are good avenues for distributing social capital, sharing and pooling resources, improving delivery of services, and strengthening school–community relations. But they can also be plagued with interorganizational politics and are difficult to sustain once funding, teams, and interest have dissipated.

The most common types of partnerships are those involving institutions of higher education and businesses, industries, and corporations. While external partners and inside school actors may share the same commitment to improving urban public high schools, both sides operate in accordance with their own organizational cultures, goals, interests, and logics of sociopolitical relations. The most effective partnerships are those where institutional representatives have good working relations and egalitarian political arrangements. Power sharing, mutual trust, and communal identification characterize relations among those who are directly involved (Kuh & Whitt, 1998; Slater, 1996).

Ineffective multi-institutional partnerships have divisive politics and interorganizational conflict over who owns schools and ought to plan and control initiatives, and they disregard the fact that, in the end, it is principals and teachers who implement and maintain programs. Reenvisioning planning and implementation processes needs to take such fundamental facts of schooling into account.

Reenvisioning

Urban public high school reforms may take the form of classroom-based initiatives, whole-school endeavors, or district-wide overhauls. They may be top-down or grassroots, and initiated within or outside schools. Reforms vary in scale, intent, and origin, but all of them involve some kind of change. Although change is often billed as positive, it can be tumultuous, painful, and unintentionally destructive. It is neither easy nor necessarily advisable.

Be that as it may, there is a need to reenvision urban public high school reform possibilities with much more attention being given to the challenges of schooling in racially, ethnically, and socioeconomically diverse communities. As Payne (2008) observes, most discussions of reform are "dangerously disconnected from the daily realities of urban schools, especially the bottom-tier schools" (p. 5). Successful reform depends on change processes with ends and means that are more directly connected to and cognizant of school organizational realities and the characteristics of urban communities. Change processes have to include principals and teachers, the people who actually work with students, and will not produce good results unless strong social infrastructures are put into place (Fullan, 2007). Reforms fail when they do not include the best, most qualified, and most directly affected people, and when school actors and stakeholders are unable to communicate or cooperate with one another. The bulk of unsuccessful initiatives can be traced to the involvement of unqualified or self-serving people, inadequate or broken social infrastructures, and seemingly intractable disputes and power struggles (Payne, 2008).

Successful reenvisioning relies on astute decisions about who is included in reform efforts and the establishment of social infrastructures that facilitate communication, decision making, and implementation. Principals must be part of change processes because of their pivotal roles in the school organizational scheme of things. They are almost always key actors in instances where reforms succeed (Sarason, 1996). Failure is likely to occur if principals and, for that matter, teachers are excluded.

Reforms are inherently political and power struggles over who should be in control are inevitable. The more types of professionals, nonprofessionals, and organizations are involved, the more decision making will be characterized by conflicts over means and ends (Sarason, 1996). Power struggles often revolve around the question of who owns the public schools: The answer is that everyone owns them and everyone should have a common interest in ensuring that all students are well educated. Reenvisioning reform depends on shared visions rooted in common interests that can be practically translated into project, program, or school-wide goals.

Another more essential question is who should own classrooms. The answer is highly qualified teachers who have the legitimate authority to do their jobs as professionals and who know how to motivate, instruct, and help students to achieve. The problem with many reforms is that teachers' authority is undermined and their professionalism is challenged to the point where their capacity to perform their roles well and effectively is greatly diminished. Outcomes very much depend on when and how teachers become part of change processes, and the extent to which qualified teachers are empowered to do their jobs.

External partners, most notably institutions of higher education, corporations, businesses, and industries can be very instrumental in the success of reforms. True reform, some argue, requires bold, ambitious multi-institutional partnerships (Zimpher & Howey, 2004). But partnerships falter when they are plagued with political intrigues, shoddy planning, mistrust, differences between organizational cultures, dissimilar goals, or poor communication (Center for Higher Educational Policy Analysis, 2005).

It is essential that qualified people with common interests in effective schooling and those directly affected by the initiative are included in planning and implementation and that in the process, power struggles are minimized. Success also rests on the development of a shared vision with clearly identified goals and sensible practices; the establishment of social infrastructures with interconnected teams and good lines of communication; and the savvy of astute managers who are able to mediate politics, facilitate communication, and coordinate the design and implementation of reforms with the fundamental facts of schooling in mind. Who needs to be involved, what visions, goals, and practices should be embraced, how planning should proceed, and what are the best strategies for implementation are essential questions with pragmatic answers.

Who Needs to Be Involved?

It goes without saying that who is appointed or volunteers to work on reform initiatives is critical for success, which depends on the involvement of qualified participants who are genuinely committed, have the expertise necessary to make meaningful contributions, get along with others, and are willing and able to roll up their sleeves to get the work done. Gate keeping is not out of the question, especially if it ensures that the best people are on board and troublesome, incompetent, or self-serving individuals are held at bay. Initiatives that are high profile, funded by large amounts of money, or viewed as career builders often attract people who are more interested in feathering their nests than doing what needs to be done to ensure success. Such people are more apt to harm rather than help the cause, especially if they attempt to seize control over deliberations. Multi-institutional partnerships are especially likely to attract individuals more interested in promoting their own agendas than contributing to the greater good of the effort as a whole.

People must also want to be involved in reform initiatives. Externally imposed directives are notoriously unsuccessful because they are forced on principals, teachers, or other school actors who are not interested in them or had no say in their conceptualization. Small-scale directives without school actor input may be put into place, but they are usually short lived and subject to "snap back" effects. School actors have a strong tendency to snap back into their former work patterns once the pressures or enforcers of initiatives have left. Major directives, such as standardized testing, have also produced less than ideal outcomes. They have given rise in many schools to teach-to-the-test modes of instruction that are deadening rather than engaging.

In all reform efforts, it is imperative that principals and the best and most qualified teachers be involved, especially the ones who are going to implement them. Efforts are bound to fail if principals and good teachers are excluded or relegated to subordinate or demeaning positions where they are not given a real

---

CONCEPT BOX 6.2

Reenvisioning: Essential Questions

1. Who needs to be involved?
2. What visions, goals, and practices should be embraced?
3. How should planning proceed?
4. What are the best strategies for implementation?

voice in what or how change should take place. Qualified teachers need to be included and respected as knowledgeable professionals.

What Visions, Goals, and Practices Should Be Embraced?

Successful reforms are guided by shared visions and have well-articulated goals with clearly identified outcomes. The purpose of many if not most urban public high school reforms is the introduction of new types of curriculum and attendant instructional and assessment practices. Such reforms are widely regarded as the best means for improving teaching and learning, and are prevalent because they can be developed and marketed outside of schools. Developers claim that change will occur only if schools and teachers adopt their curriculum and methods of instruction. Packaged curricular and instructional materials may come with sensible goals, state-of-the-art content, and carefully thought out and tested practices. But the problem with many of them is that they do not necessarily fit into the organizational contexts of urban public high schools. Curricular visions, goals, and attendant practices need to be contextualized so that they can be incorporated into classroom regimens in ways that are responsive to racially, ethnically, and socioeconomically diverse students. Contextualized programs not only require sensitivity to actual classroom dynamics, but may also entail some attention to school-wide reculturation, restructuring, or remoralization, all of which are addressed later in the chapter.

How Should Planning Proceed?

Strong and sustainable social infrastructures are imperative for effective planning. Everyone directly involved in a reform initiative should be an active participant in well-organized team infrastructures where teamwork is socially interconnected and characterized by good lines of communication. Small-scale reforms may involve only one team. Whole-school, district-wide, or other large scale reforms usually require more elaborate multitiered team infrastructures. In efforts involving multi-institutional partnerships, it is a good idea to establish a steering committee comprised of school board representatives, teacher union officials, the superintendent and school principals, as well as representatives from partnering institutions of higher education, corporations, businesses, and industries. Steering committees have oversight over the quality and funding of the reform effort, and if they are socially cohesive and meet on a regular basis, are in the best position to work out political and other issues. The actual design and implementation of reforms is accomplished by members of other teams at the center of which should be those that include the principal and qualified teachers.

Team infrastructures work best when they are coordinated by savvy managers able to mediate politics and facilitate interteam communication. Managers need release time, resources, and other kinds of support that will allow them to devote significant time and attention to the endeavor. They may report to steering committees or whoever is in charge of the reform, and are ideally involved in the reform from its inception all the way through implementation.

What Are the Best Strategies for Implementation?

Effective strategies for implementing reform ultimately boil down to the local decisions and choices that actually determine how initiatives are put into place (Sarason, 1996). Local decision and choices make the difference between success and failure regardless of the types of planned innovations or educational practices. They determine whether or not teachers will adopt the changes and sustain them over time. Sarason (1996) and his associates in their studies of implementation strategies found that the most effective ones were consonant with the local decision making, motivations and needs of teachers. Ineffective strategies relied too heavily on outside consultants, one-shot preimplementation training, pay for training, formal evaluations, or they were overly comprehensive.

Effective strategies are those that promote mutual adaptation where initiatives are adapted to the realities of schools while, at the same time, teachers and administrators are adapting their practices to the initiative (Sarason, 1996). They provide teachers with timely feedback and substantive professional development. They also give principals and teachers the ways and means to correct errors and fix problems. The strategies that are most effective, especially when they are used in concert, are:

- Concrete, teacher-specific, and extended professional development
- Provision of classroom assistance
- Teacher observations of similar initiatives in other classrooms
- Regular team meetings that focus on implementation strategies and problem solving
- Teacher participation in implementation decisions
- Principal participation in professional development

The importance of principals during and after implementation cannot be overstated. They provide moral support and give legitimacy to initiatives. Teachers are unlikely to stick with change without the support and legitimization provided by principals because it is they who will ultimately determine the fate of reforms.

Reformers also need to recognize that change, especially at the classroom level, involves loss, anxiety, and emotional pain. This is especially true for veteran teachers with many years of teaching experience. Senior teachers are the most likely to snap back into their old modes of instruction after the hoopla of implementation is over. Teachers who are not involved in local decisions and choices often feel disempowered or alienated. Their emotional reactions to change may be similar to grieving processes following death or other major life events (Kübler-Ross, 1970). Principals and managers of implementation need to be mindful of the strong feelings that teachers and others have about unsettling the status quo. Since emotions permeate the entire change process, having a clear and intentional affective message is vital and often more important than logical explanations or justifications (Gibson & Barsade, 2003). Leaders of change need to be able to lead in emotionally intelligent ways (Palmer, Walls, Burgess, & Stough, 2001).

Reformers also need to recognize that it can take years to implement and institutionalize change. The problem with many reform efforts is that people lose interest in them if they are not carried out quickly. Another problem is that participants come and go and this may slow down or derail momentum. But the most enduring pillars of the long-term success of urban high school reform are not planning or implementation processes but, rather, school culture, structure, and moral orders.

Reculturation

School organizational culture is at the crux of the problem and process of change (Sarason, 1996). The long-term success of urban public high school reform depends on school cultures which are comprised of the understandings that have the most significant influence on how school actors define their roles, form organizational identities, and render schooling into meaningful and actionable practices. Successful reform may depend on *reculturation* aimed at the production of school cultures that enable principals and teachers to construct and sustain professional roles, strong identification with their schools, effective schooling practices, and mutually supportive relations.

A useful way to conceive reculturation processes is to break the definition of school organizational culture into three layers (Gibson & Barsade, 2003). The top layer includes the visible aspects of cultural understandings—behaviors, practices, projections of individual and group identity, language, styles of dress, and other outwardly apparent expressions.

CONCEPT BOX 6.3

Reculturation

Reculturation is the production of school cultures that enable principals and teachers to construct, and sustain, professional roles, strong identification with their schools, effective schooling practices, and mutually supportive relations.

The second layer is comprised of less visible behavioral norms, especially those related to how school actors are expected to appropriately define and carry out their roles. Norms are the unspoken behavioral rules that school actors apply to professional conduct, conflict, and airing of differences, emotions, political maneuverings, communication, and other actions and interactions within and between groups and individuals. They sustain cultures, for better or worse, through social rewards and sanctions. Behaviors regarded as appropriate are encouraged and rewarded while those considered to be inappropriate are punished. Norms set the terms and boundaries for how people are expected to perform their roles and handle relations and are thus a powerful form of social control (O'Reilly & Chatman, 1996). School actors are much more likely to abide by prevailing norms if they garner social acceptance, approval, or a sense of belonging and will do so even if their actions undermine good educational practice. They go with the normative flow because they want to fit in.

The third and deepest layer of school culture includes the values, beliefs, and assumptions about how schooling works. Deep-seated values are especially critical because they may emphasize individual autonomy over teamwork, entrenched tradition over innovation, or fierce competition rather than constructive collaboration. Values are the tacit foundation of the other two cultural layers. Even though they may be internalized to the point where school actors are unable to articulate them, they have a profound bearing on how school actors respond to school operations (Schein, 1991).

Reculturation depends on changing elements of school culture at all three levels, which is why it is so difficult to accomplish. Like all cultural processes, reculturation is a social construction. It is a production created and maintained by people during the course of ongoing relations and interactions. Reculturation is also very political as people vie for power and control over outward expressions, norms, and values. Controlling cultural processes is a politically consequential means for acquiring social control.

Subcultures must also be addressed. Reculturation is not possible in schools torn apart by administrator or teacher factions with subcultures that make it impossible for school actors to construct shared cultural commitments. Veteran teachers, especially those with vested interests in preserving an existing culture, may clash with principals, new teachers, and others who want change. Their subcultures can be quite tenacious and obstructionist, which makes matters even worse.

There are ways to facilitate reculturation that bridge the old with the new. An example is drawn from my own work and collaborative research with a principal and teachers involved in the establishment of a new science, technology, engineering, and mathematics (STEM) urban public high school (Rhodes, Stevens, & Hemmings, 2011). Over 86% of students enrolled in the school are Black. Twenty-eight percent have special needs and 84% receive free and reduced lunches. The plan for the new school, which involved a multi-institutional partnership, was to implement state-of-the art STEM programs that would serve underrepresented groups and be a beacon for other urban schools. An instructional planning team was formed that included the school principal, five highly qualified lead teachers in science, technology, mathematics, social studies, and English, and me, an embedded university researcher.

The planning team understood at the outset that the key to fostering educational success was the production of a positive school culture that engendered relational trust, built community, facilitated communication, and supported rigorous and innovative project-based curriculum and instruction. Members' understanding of the critical importance of school culture was supported by research (Fullan, 2001, 2007; Goodlad, 1975; Joyce, Hersh, & McKibbon, 1983; Lortie, 1975; Rutter, Maughan, Mortimore, & Ouston, 1979; Sarason, 1996), and their own wisdom of practice gleaned from years of experience. They understood that positive school culture is guided by a clear vision, intentionally instilled core values, and incorporation of cultural commitments into the selection and induction of new staff.

Planning team members began their school cultural production by constructing their own norms which they posted on the wall of their workspace. Among these norms were those that emphasized the importance of "doing what we say we will do"; "respecting members' time, opinions, materials, personalities and learning styles"; and sharing all concerns "with the team or not at all." The team brought in consultants, including one from the state department of education who encouraged members to work backwards from a clear vision of the new school to curriculum and instructional strategies. The team decided that college readiness through project-based learning would be the overriding vision and they developed core values—courage, respect, empathy, desire, integrity, and teamwork—to support it. The values were defined in clear and simple language and instilled during principal and teacher hiring processes, professional development, student summer bridge programs, orientations, and other means. There was a public relations campaign when the school year began that promoted the values. Colorful posters that displayed the values were hung on the walls in classrooms and corridors. Teachers worked with students to make sure core values were understood and put into practice. And staff frequently referenced the values during parent and student conferences.

Core values were also a critical part of the selection criteria used in teacher hiring processes. Planning team members were instrumental in hiring the teaching staff for the new school. The hiring process involved:

- *Teacher selection panel* where the planning team teachers performed interviews along with the principal;
- *Interview questions* designed to assess strength and fit with the new school's vision and core values; and

- *Collaborative team tasks* where two candidates performed an interactive task involving communication and collaboration skills in a "fishbowl" environment in front of the principal and teacher selection panel.

The process was dubbed "T2" interviews; they were intense and regarded by the planning team as the beginning of cultural induction for new teachers. The next step was to socialize new teachers into the school culture through team-building and professional development. There was an informal mixer at a local restaurant aimed at merging the planning team teachers, all of whom were veterans with many years of experience, with the cadre of new teachers. The idea was to head off the formation of factions and subcultures that could derail efforts to forge a shared school culture.

The merged teachers participated in summer professional development at an outdoor education center facilitated by staff adept at team-building through the use of kinesthetic, discovery, and developmental activities. Veteran planning team teachers and new teachers got to know each other at a much deeper level, including their family stories and their learning and communication styles. There were trust-building games where group members had to lean on each other both emotionally and physically. Nine more days of professional development ensued and included intense training in project-based learning, technology software and hardware tools, and social–emotional learning. Decisions were also hammered out in regard to scheduling, discipline, uniforms, and cell phones.

There were only freshmen during the first year of the new school with plans to add a grade each year until a final configuration of six grades, 7 through 12, was achieved. The principal and first-year teachers were aware that as each grade was added they would have to split up and work with each new cohort of teachers and students to pass on and sustain the culture. They formed teacher teams to accomplish this and also to facilitate collaborative teamwork in the development of project-based pedagogy.

Reculturation also needs to address student youth culture and subcultures. Students in multiracial and multiethnic urban high schools typically form racially and ethnically diverse cliques with socially thick boundaries. Clique members produce and express subcultures with distinct styles of speech, dress, and behavioral codes intended to set themselves off from, or signal opposition to, other cliques and groups. When intergroup relations are strained, bullying, victimization, and fights for respect and dominance become prevalent. Gendered antagonisms also surface and are often expressed through verbal and physical sexual harassment (Hemmings, 2002).

Youth hostilities blight school culture. Advisory groups or other small-group systems where students learn and practice social and emotional learning (SEL) skills can be very effective in mitigating hostilities. Students' capacity to build productive relationships is enhanced by SEL skills which can also contribute to healthier attitudes toward learning and academic success (Elias et al., 1997; Zins & Elias, 2007). They include skills related to the development of empathy, appreciation of other cultures and perspectives, impulse control, conflict resolution, responsibility, and assisting rather than harassing peers. Required advisory classes with SEL curriculum can be included in students' schedules. The Collaborative for Academic, Social, and Emotional Learning (CASEL) provides valuable resources for teachers and other school staff members who facilitate such classes (www.casel.org). If the curriculum of these classes is tied to the overall vision and core values of the school, they can be a powerful force for reculturation that changes classroom dynamics, as well as student corridor life, throughout the school.

Culturally responsive teaching (CRT) may also improve student attitudes and engagement in schooling. Geneva Gay (2000) offers useful insights on how CRT can enhance the school performance of students of color who embrace cultures that clash with school culture and other cultures. Black, Chicano, Latino, Asian, American Indian, and other racially and ethnically diverse students may perform better on multiple measures if curriculum and instruction is filtered through their own cultures and cultural frames of reference. Key features of CRT include teacher acceptance and affirmation of cultural differences, teacher caring, multicultural curriculum, and culturally responsive classroom discourse.

The effectiveness of CRT may be enhanced by explicit attention to the resistance of Black, Chicano, and other involuntary minority youth from historically marginalized groups who embrace oppositional cultural frames of reference in response to generations of discrimination and inequitable access to educational and economic opportunities (Fordham, 1988, 1996, 2008; Fordham & Ogbu, 1986; Matute-Bianchi, 1991; Ogbu, 1978, 1987; Ogbu & Simons, 1998). And attention may also have to be paid to the sociocultural influences of urban street gangs (Garot, 2010).

Reculturation may also be facilitated through the utilization of paraeducators, voluntary mentors, and other intermediaries who perform auxiliary roles as translators, counselors, tutors, and cultural brokers who help bridge cultural differences (Rueda & DeNeve, 1999). Because intermediaries are not restricted to classrooms and do not evaluate or otherwise judge student achievement, they are in a good position to connect racially, ethnically, and socioeconomically diverse students to a wider spectrum of social and cultural capital and other avenues for advancement. They can help youths to navigate the "unfamiliar territory" of Anglo/European American middle-class schooling and society in ways that teachers cannot do (Ernst-Slavit & Wenger, 2006).

I conducted a study of a school-to-work program in an urban public high school that employed intermediaries (Hemmings, 2007). The program was located in a school that served mostly low-income Black students, and the intermediaries, known as youth advocates, assisted students with internship job placements. They also sought to increase students' educational attainments through concerted efforts to help students acquire the cultural and social capital they needed to go to college. They facilitated the acquisition of cultural capital through "reality therapy" where they acknowledged the importance of neighborhood survival skills, emphasized positive life choices, and guided socially and geographically isolated students into the unfamiliar territory of college. They connected students to social capital by linking them to educational resources and White, middle-class social networks. A number of students were in desperate need of psychiatric counseling, legal assistance, or someone to help them with abusive family members, unwanted pregnancies, or the birth of their children. Youth advocates stepped in, connected students to social services, and helped them to navigate legal, medical, and judicial institutions.

Reculturation may be crucial to the success of urban public high school reform, but it might not be possible without restructuring. Reculturation usually goes hand-in-hand with restructuring.

Restructuring

Reforms that focus on restructuring, especially those conducive to the production of positive school cultures, may entail a number of changes, especially those related to formal roles and responsibilities, professional community teams, scheduling, and governance. Urban public high schools are structurally semibureaucratic in ways that could allow school actors, especially teachers, to assume more professionally empowering roles and responsibilities. They have loosely coupled activity structures that can be restructured so that teachers can be leaders who support each other's professional development and collaborate in the development of effective pedagogies. Urban public high schools are also sites where flexible scheduling and governance with shared decision making may be quite advantageous.

Principals and teachers in many urban high schools assume many roles with myriad responsibilities that go well beyond their formal job descriptions as administrators or classroom educators. The demands on them are enormous, and yet they are not necessarily accorded the professional status or power they need to perform their roles and responsibilities in optimal ways. Their positions

---

CONCEPT BOX 6.4

Restructuring

Restructuring involves structural changes in schooling systems especially those related to formal roles and responsibilities, professional community teams, scheduling, and governance.

are constantly being questioned or undermined when, in fact, they should be shored up within school organizational structures that empower them to be professionals working together in professional communities.

Urban public high schools can be restructured so that qualified teachers can be leaders in whole-school or classroom reform. Schools' loosely coupled activity structures provide school actors with some degree of autonomy to develop and deploy technologies related to work processes (Meyer & Rowan, 1983). Unfortunately, teacher isolation is the norm in most urban high schools where faculty members are left alone to come up with their own repertoire of instructional strategies that they seldom share or make public. Reward structures reinforce this by placing most of the responsibility for feedback and accountability on students rather than principals and colleagues (Lieberman & Miller, 2004). Teachers are subject to the logic of confidence where principals, parents, and others trust them to do their jobs without direct supervision, and where accountability may be largely based on student standardized test scores.

Teacher isolation needs to end so that pedagogical strategies can be coproduced and disseminated, and accountability may be based more on peer assessment involving constructive feedback rather than test scores with punitive sanctions. Such systems are characterized by different levels of teacher qualifications where the most certifiably capable and experienced senior lead teachers work with new and less experienced teachers, and all teachers are working together as teams. This is how professional teachers can perform their roles and carry out responsibilities in professional communities that actually support quality instruction.

Qualified senior lead teachers are vital in such structures. Lead teachers have demonstrable leadership qualities, good communication skills, a consistent pattern of professional growth, an observable ability to collaborate with others, and a strong commitment to teaching as a career and profession. All of these characteristics can be nurtured and assessed throughout teachers' careers in programs with peer mentors or coaches. Teachers can progress through levels from apprentice, learner, advanced, to lead teachers in programs where they are assisted and evaluated by higher-level peers. Lead teachers and principals can be part of review panels to which struggling teachers are referred. Panels can assign consulting teachers to help referred teachers improve their instructional skills or, if improvements do not transpire, recommend nonrenewal of the teacher's contract.

Professional communities, which ideally take the form of school-based teacher teams, are not only a structural feature necessary for lead teachers to work with less experienced colleagues, but also for all teachers to work together in the coproduction of effective pedagogies. Teacher team structures can be especially effective in urban high schools that serve youths from diverse cultural backgrounds, socioeconomic locations, needs, and emotional and cognitive characteristics. Student diversity makes it virtually impossible for high school teachers to come up with technologies that work for all students all of the time. It poses monumental challenges for isolated teachers who do not have the support of more experienced teachers. Teams with both lead and more novice teachers representing core subject matter areas, and who work with the same group of students, are in a much better position to develop and adjust pedagogical practices in their classroom regimens. In order to accommodate teacher teams, schedules should include time for common team planning and also be flexible enough for teachers to engage in team-teaching or other strategies for putting innovative pedagogies into practice. Block or other types of flexible scheduling are ideal for this (Queen, 2008).

High schools also have tracking structures where students are scheduled into different classes with differentiated curriculums that vary significantly in terms of their nature, meanings, and practices. Most have academic or occupational tracking where students are categorized as fast, average, or slow learners on the basis of test scores and past performance and assigned to low-level (e.g., special education and remedial), regular-level, or upper-level (e.g., honors and Advanced Placement) classes (Oakes, 1985). This structure reinforces social inequalities as students of color from the lowest rungs of the socioeconomic ladder are typically more likely than White middle-class students to be assigned to low-level classes. Tracking may continue to be a feature of urban public high schools, but it, too, can be restructured. More progressive and just forms of tracking provide underperforming students with chances to improve their performances to the point where they can be moved into more advanced classes that are more academically empowering. This not only may entail effective academic interventions, but also explicit instruction in the particular sets of skills, knowledge, discourses, and other cultural practices that define what it means to be an educated person in U.S. society (Levinson & Holland, 1996). Immigrant, racial, and ethnic minority students can be better exposed to the cultural criteria for what it takes to be identified as more or less educated (Delpit, 1995). And they can be encouraged to form academic identities in ways that affirm, add to, or complement their cultural identities. This can be done in restructured tracking systems that are socially and culturally responsive.

Restructuring reforms, especially those that go hand-in-hand with reculturation should foster the establishment of governance structures that include teachers in shared decision making. These structures most ideally are negotiated as part of union contracts. A good example is the instructional leadership team (ILT) model included in the union contract for Cincinnati Public Schools. The contract stipulates that all schools in the district establish an ILT so that the principal, teachers, and other members may share leadership and make decisions in the following areas:

- To develop, review, and evaluate instructional programs;
- To monitor and improve school operations and procedures that impact instruction;

- To plan and monitor training of staff;
- To develop and monitor the school budget;
- To create and maintain a safe and orderly school environment;
- To oversee the formation of teams in team-based schools within given parameters;
- To perform all other responsibilities assigned by this contract to the ILT;
- Meet to review budget and implementation of ILT decisions quarterly. (Cincinnati Federation of Teachers, 2009)

The membership of ILTs includes the principal, up to two assistant principals, two parent representatives, two nonteaching staff members; and teacher members who are serving as the school's union representative, program facilitators, a lead teacher for special education, and other teachers representing academic departments and specialist areas. The contract spells out the structure and operations of ILTs including voting procedures, subcommittees, meeting agendas and minutes, training, policies and practices, and parallel structures.

Teacher teams coupled with school leadership teams like ILTs can be institutionalized and sustained through schedules that include common planning times. But their effectiveness may depend on school moral orders.

Remoralization

As Fullan (2007) observes, true change involves shared meanings with moral and intellectual dimensions.

> Making a difference in the lives of students requires care, commitment, and passion as well as the intellectual know-how to do something about it. Moral purpose and knowledge are the two main change forces that drive success (Fullan, 2007, p. 21).

School actors in demoralized urban public high schools lack moral purpose. They are vested in the failure of others because it essentially frees them from taking responsibility or being morally responsible for students. Teachers who work hard and get remarkable results are treated like deviant "rate busters" because they set a pace that makes other teachers look bad (Payne, 2008, p. 22). Rate-buster teachers do not abide by prevalent norms of failure and, like deviants in other organizational settings, are socially ostracized or negatively sanctioned. They learn not to talk about what they do effectively and minimize contact with colleagues and otherwise marginalize themselves (Kozol, 1967; Rosenfeld, 1971).

Demoralized urban high schools are places where highly qualified teachers are unable to perform their roles as professionals in professional communities. These schools are plagued with an insidious sense of futility, pessimism, distrust, and disengagement. Instruction is uncoordinated and uninspiring, and resources are lacking and badly utilized. Curriculum is narrow, boring, and watered down. Promising programs and good personnel come and go (Payne, 2008).

Demoralized schools are also tainted by what Payne (2008) describes as the "principle of negative interpretation" where everything people do is interpreted in the most negative way possible.

> If parents don't show up at school, what does it mean? That they don't care. If a colleague fails to make hall duty, what does it mean? That she's blowing off her responsibility. If a principal fails to observe classes? She doesn't care about the kids. But if parents do show up? They're just coming to stick their noses in our business. If the colleague shows up for hall duty? Sucking up to the principal. If the principal does start doing observations? She's just trying to impress the people downtown—and why is she just starting now. If a teacher is really nice to students, they must take that as proof she thinks they're dumb and won't hold them to standards. If she's mean? Racist bitch. (Payne, 2008, p. 25)

Demoralized schools are fertile grounds for warring factions. Older teachers become pitted against younger ones. Constructivist, inquiry-oriented teachers battle with more teacher-centered traditional ones. Spanish-speaking teachers lock horns with English-speaking ones. Race and ethnicity are almost always implicated in factions as well as other aspects of school life. Everything is racialized.

Remoralization in urban public high schools may be critical and very likely imperative for reform. The process involves concerted efforts to build relational trust so that morally purposeful exchanges can actually take place between school actors. Relational trust is organized around sets of role relationships: teachers with students, teachers with other teachers, teachers with parents, and with their school principal (Bryk & Schneider, 2002). Each person in the relationship has an understanding of his or her role obligations and holds expectations about the role obligations of others. Relational trust breaks down when individuals perceive that the people they are working with are not behaving in ways consistent with their obligations. Trust depends on what behaviors people observe, and whether these behaviors are interpreted as consistent with expectations associated with responsibilities.

The criteria for discerning appropriate behaviors necessary for relational trust are respect, competence, personal regard and care for others, and integrity. These criteria advance the interests of children and are the essential ingredients of the ethical and moral commitments school actors ought to have. As Oakes, Quartz, Ryan, and Lipton (1999) observed in their research:

> [Unless teachers] were bound together by a moral commitment to growth, empathy, and shared responsibility, [they] were as likely to replicate the

prevailing school culture as to change it. Unless they applied their collaboration to educative, caring, socially just, and participatory activities they continued to closely guard their classroom autonomy, be suspicious of the capacity of teaming to divide and balkanize their faculty, and distrust collaboration with those outside the school. (Oakes et al, 1999, p. 285)

Morality and sound educational ethics are the cultural components of schools' moral orders that should guide the right way for school actors to realize educational goals (Metz, 1978; Selznick, 1992). In moralized schools, school actors work together in the service of an ethically justifiable moral order to which everyone owes allegiance. Such an order is comprised of meanings and practices that promote good and equitable educational opportunities.

Moral orders are formed and ultimately enacted during the course of everyday school relations and they are affected by the moral–ethical commitments of administrators and teachers. Sometimes they are intentionally created, like the "moral contracts" that Sizer and Sizer (1999) include in their agenda for school reform. More often than not, they are constructed and sustained in more informally reinforced ways. They carry moral overtones that are detected by school actors as they absorb, make, or contest understandings that are supposed to make sure they are "good" administrators, teachers, students, and staff. These overtones may cause teachers to believe they have done something wrong if they fail to instruct in a certain way or students to feel guilty if they do not work hard. Or they may be toned down or challenged by school actors who cannot or will not abide by them. School actors in any case infuse their own personal moral–ethical commitments into their responses (and allegiance) to their school's moral order. And they do so in reaction to pressures from peers, the surrounding community, and other external sources. They are collectively into the moral order or splintered out of it.

Moral orders can be broken down into three dimensions—worthwhile curriculum, proper pedagogy, and good character—that can be used to analyze demoralized schools and applied in remoralization processes (Hemmings, 2006a). Moral overtones are emphasized in these dimensions through the use of adjectives such as *worthwhile*, *proper*, and *good* and auxiliary verbs like *should* and *ought*. The curriculum dimension in the moral order should include beliefs

---

CONCEPT BOX 6.5

Remoralization

Remoralization entails the institutionalization of moral orders infused with sound educational ethics for worthwhile curriculum, proper pedagogy, and good character to which school actors owe allegiance.

about what ought to constitute worthwhile content; that is, academic knowledge, skills, and cultural understandings that nurture individual potential, create genuine opportunities for young people to live good, meaningful lives, provide access to educational and economic opportunities, and "guarantee unity and equity in American education" (Metz, 1990, p. 83). Urban public high schools should offer a full and rich slate of science, mathematics, language arts, social studies, foreign language, art, music, and other classes, and teachers should feel they have a moral obligation to deliver curriculum that is universally valued and equitably empowering.

Proper pedagogy pertains to the norms and conventions that structure standards and practices for instruction, assessment, and discipline. Ethically justifiable pedagogy upholds high standards, and includes practices that effectively convey worthwhile curriculum, assess students' performance fairly and in ways that improve achievement, and ensures authentic learning. It also includes disciplinary practices that maintain order and promote good character. Improper pedagogies that are ethically unjustifiable feed into defensive teaching where worthwhile curriculum is watered down or eliminated, students are barraged with mindless fill-in-the-blank worksheets, and practices related to instruction, assessment, and discipline are essentially exercises in educational pointlessness.

The last dimension of school moral order embodies cultural values about what it means to have and express good character. Such values should foster the cultivation of character that is marked by "goodness and excellence, stability and discipline" and other "virtuous" traits (Rosario, 2000, p. 39). Virtuous traits not only make individual school actors better people, but also are necessary for maintaining school relations that are civil, mutually respectful, and responsible. Good character is also distinguished by expressions of care at the heart of morally interdependent and genuinely responsive school relations (Noddings, 1984, 1999).

Remoralization in the final analysis may be and often is a necessary complement to reculturation and restructuring in urban public high school reform. All three components should be considered in reenvisioned planning and implementation efforts. And all possibilities for reform must be mindful of the fundamental facts of schooling which ultimately boil down to how a high quality of life and learning is actually produced in classrooms.

Summation

Successful urban public high school reform initiatives take into account fundamental facts of schooling. The most consequential fact is classroom dynamics. Initiatives eventually trickle down into classrooms where teachers in their relations with students produce the schoolwork regimens with the most direct effects on teaching and learning. It is also a fact that life in classrooms is wrought by school organizational cultures comprised of outward expressions, behavioral norms, and deep-seated values. School cultures are socially constructed within semibureaucratic structures for defining roles and responsibilities, technologies related to work processes, scheduling, governance, and other systems. Urban public high schools also have moral orders with moral and ethical overtones for worthwhile curriculum, proper pedagogy, and good character. Principal leadership is an especially pivotal fact of schooling. Principals as apex administrators can wield significant power and influence over school cultures, structures, and moral orders. They are usually key actors in successful school reforms. Another fundamental fact is local community characteristics. The cultural and socioeconomic characteristics of surrounding urban neighborhoods have a profound bearing on schools' relations with parents and other community members as well as students' commitment to formal schooling. Federal, state, and school district directives are facts that can help or hurt school–community relations and other aspects of schooling. Their originators do not necessarily factor in the operational realities and contexts of urban schools, and generally are not held accountable for results. Finally, multi-institutional partnerships are an increasingly common fact of schooling that can support reform efforts through the pooling of resources, social networks, strengthening school–community relations and other means, but also undermine much-needed change through interorganizational politics.

The planning and implementation of urban public high school reform should be reenvisioned in ways that recognize the fundamental facts of schooling. Most discussions of reform are dangerously disconnected from actual school operations. Reenvisioned change processes are driven by practical, reality-based answers to the questions of who needs to be involved; what visions, goals, and practices should be embraced; how planning should proceed; and what are the best strategies for implementation. Principals, teachers, and other school actors most directly affected by reform initiatives are chief among those who need to be included on planning teams. Successful reforms are guided by shared visions, well articulated goals, and clearly identified outcomes that are contextualized so they can be practically incorporated into administrative offices and classroom regimens. Planning processes cannot proceed unless there are strong and sustainable social infrastructures with well-organized teams, interconnected modes of teamwork, and good lines of communication. It also helps to have a good manager who has the know-how, release time, resources, and political savvy to steer initiatives through from beginning to end.

The most effective implementation strategies ultimately boil down to the local decisions and choices that determine how an initiative is actually put into place. Such strategies promote mutual adaptation where reforms are adapted to the realities of schools as school actors are adapting their practices to the initiatives. Power struggles during planning and implementation, especially around the question of who owns schools and classrooms, may also have to be settled. Everyone involved in urban public high school reforms should have a common political interest in making sure that all students are well educated and that qualified teachers educate students well.

School organizational culture is at the crux of the problem and processes of change and reculturation may be necessary for change to occur. Reculturation processes are geared toward the production of positive school cultures that enable principals and teachers to construct and sustain professional roles, maintain strong identification with their school, use effective practices, and have mutually supportive relations. Processes take place at three levels—visible outward expressions, hidden behavioral norms, and deep-seated values. Overall school culture may be targeted, but reculturation may also involve the mediation of administrator, teacher, and student faction subcultures. Positive school cultures are not possible in schools torn apart by administrator and teacher factions or rivalries between student cliques. Concerted efforts need to be made to recruit, hire, and retain teachers who commit themselves to a shared positive culture, and also to mediate and merge factions. It may also be necessary to address intergroup student hostilities. Good strategies include advisory classes or other kinds of small-group systems where students learn and practice social and emotional learning. Culturally responsive teaching and the utilization of para-educators, voluntary mentors, or other intermediaries may also be useful.

Restructuring often goes hand-in-hand with reculturation, especially structural changes related to formal roles and responsibilities, professional community teams, scheduling, and governance. An advantage of the fact that urban public high schools are semibureaucratic is that their loosely coupled activity structures provide administrators and teachers with some autonomy to be leaders and collaborators in the development and execution of effective pedagogies. They can perform their roles and responsibilities as true professionals working together in professional communities in teams that meet on a regular basis during scheduled common planning times. Teacher isolation is replaced with teaming and reward structures based more on peer assessment that involves constructive feedback rather than student standardized test scores. These systems have different levels of teacher qualifications where the most certifiably capable and experienced lead teachers work with new and less experienced teachers, and all teachers work together on teams that are responsible for the instruction of the same group of students. Governance may also need to be restructured so there is shared decision making, most ideally through contractually negotiated school leadership teams where principals, teachers, and other members share leadership and make decisions about instructional programs, school operations, staff training, school budget, orderly school environments, team formation, and other areas.

Academic and occupational tracking that reinforces socioeconomic inequalities should also be restructured. More progressive and socially just forms of tracking are those that provide underperforming students with chances to improve their performances so they can be moved into more advanced classes.

This may entail explicit instruction in the cultural criteria for what it means to be an educated person in the United States.

Finally, true change rests on shared moral purpose. Many urban public high schools are demoralized to the point where administrators, teachers, and students are vested in their own failure and the failure of others. They are places where good teachers are unable to perform their roles as professionals in professional communities, and where there is a pervasive sense of futility, pessimism, distrust, disengagement, and curricular and instructional malaise.

Urban high schools can be remoralized through the construction and institutionalization of an ethically justifiable moral order to which all school actors owe allegiance. Such orders carry moral overtones about what it means to have "worthwhile" curriculum, "proper" pedagogy, and "good" character in urban public high schools that serve racially, ethnically, and socioeconomically diverse students. We have a moral and ethical obligation as a society to provide all adolescents regardless of their backgrounds with the education they need to live good, meaningful lives and gain access to educational and occupational opportunities. We have the same obligation to teach young people to be good citizens in a democracy that values and supports public high schools, including those in demographically diverse and economically impoverished urban areas.

Possibilities for Urban Public High School Reform

Discussion Questions

1. If you were hired as a consultant for reforming a troubled urban public high school, what advice would you provide?
2. Teacher unions are often criticized for undermining urban high school reform. What can they do to help the cause?
3. Should urban public high school reform be largely bottom-up and site-based or put into the hands of school boards and district officials? Why or why not?
4. What role should national, state, and local politicians, legislators, policymakers, and other outsiders play in urban public high school reform efforts?
5. What is the most effective or best way for multi-institutional partnerships to contribute to reform efforts?
6. The bottom line in all school reform is classroom dynamics. How can teachers be empowered to more effectively instruct, assess, and discipline students who are racially, ethnically, and socioeconomically diverse, have special needs, and come to school with a wide range of motivation and attitudes toward formal schooling?

REFERENCES

Adams, N. G. (1999). Fighting to be somebody: Resisting erasure and the discursive practices of female adolescent fighting. *Educational Studies, 30*(2), 115–139.

Anderson, C. G. (1992). Behaviors of the most effective and least effective school board members. *ERS Spectrum, 10*, 15–18.

Anderson, E. (1998). The codes of the street. In L. C. Mahdi, N. G. Christopher, & M. Meade (Eds.), *Crossroads: The quest for contemporary rites of passage* (pp. 91–97). Chicago, IL: Open Court.

Andrews, D. J. C. (2009). The construction of Black high-achiever identities in a predominantly white high school. *Anthropology & Education Quarterly, 40*(3), 297–317.

Appleton, N. (1983). *Cultural pluralism in education: Theoretical foundations.* New York, NY: Longman.

Au, K. H. (1980). Participant structures in a reading lesson with Hawaiian children: Analysis of a culturally appropriate instructional event. *Anthropology & Education Quarterly, 11*(2), 91–115.

Bankston, C. L., & Caldas, S. J. (2009). *Public education—America's civil religion: A social history.* New York, NY: Teachers College Press.

Baratz, S. S., & Baratz, J. C. (1970). Early childhood intervention: The social science base of institutional racism. *Harvard Educational Review, 40*, 29–49.

Berger, P. L., & Luckmann, T. (1967). *The social construction of reality: A treatise in the sociology of knowledge.* Garden City, NY: Anchor Books.

Bernstein, B. (1971). *Class, codes, and control* (Vol. 1). London: Routledge & Kegan Paul.

Bettis, P. J. (1996). Urban students, liminality, and the postindustrial context. *Sociology of Education, 69*, 105–125.

Blau, P. (1974). *On the nature of organizations.* New York, NY: Wiley.

Blumer, H. (1969). *Symbolic interactionism: Perspective and method.* Englewood Cliffs, NJ: Prentice-Hall.

Bourdieu, P. (1977). *Outline of a theory of practice.* Cambridge, England: Cambridge University Press.

Bourdieu, P., & Passeron, J. (1990). *Reproduction in education, society and culture.* Thousand Oaks, CA: Sage.

Bowles, S., & Gintis, H. (1976). *Schooling in capitalist America.* New York, NY: Basic Books.

Brake, M. (1980). *The sociology of youth culture and youth subculture.* London: Routledge & Kegan Paul.

Brake, M. (1985). *Comparative youth culture: The sociology of youth culture and youth subcultures in America, Britain, and Canada.* London: Routledge & Kegan Paul.

Brubaker, R. (2004). Rethinking classical theory: The sociological vision of Pierre Bourdieu. In D. L. Swartz & V. L. Zolberg (Eds.), *After Bourdieu: Influence, critique, elaboration* (pp. 25–64). Dordrecht, the Netherlands: Kluwer.

Bryk, A. S., & Schneider, B. (2002). *Trust in schools: A core resource for improvement.* New York, NY: Russell Sage Foundation.

Butterfield, S. P. (2006). To be young, gifted, and somewhat foreign: The role of ethnicity in Black student achievement. In E. M. Horvat & C. O'Connor (Eds.), *Beyond acting white: Reframing the debate on Black student achievement* (pp. 133–155). Lanham, MD: Rowman & Littlefield.

Caldas, S. J., & Bankston, C. L. (2008, January) A re-analysis of the legal, political and social landscape of desegregation from *Plessy v. Ferguson* to *Community Schools v. Seattle School District No. 1 Et Al. Brigham Young University Education and Law Journal, 1,* 217–256.

Cammarota, J, (2008). The cultural organizing of youth ethnographers: Formalizing a praxis-based pedagogy. *Anthropology & Education Quarterly, 39*(1), 45–58.

Carnegie Corporation. (1986). *A nation prepared: Teachers for the 21st century.* Hyattsville, MD: Carnegie Forum on Education and the Economy.

Carol, L. N., Cunningham, L. L., Danzberger, J. P., Kirst, M. W., McCloud, B. A., & Usdan, M. D. (1986). *School boards: Strengthening grassroots leadership.* Washington, DC: Institute for Educational Leadership.

Carspecken, P. F. (2002). The hidden history of praxis theory within critical ethnography and criticalism/postmodernism problematic. In Y. Zou & E. T. Trueba (Eds.), *Ethnography and schools: Qualitative approaches to the study of education* (pp. 55–86). Lanham, MD: Rowman & Littlefield.

Center for Higher Education Policy Analysis. (2005). *The opportunities and challenges of partnering with schools.* Los Angeles, CA: University of Southern California.

Cincinnati Federation of Teachers (2009). Cincinnati Federation of Teachers Collective Bargaining Agreement. Retrieved from http://www.cft-aft.org/pdf/CFT%20CBA.pdf

Cohen, S. (1980). *Folk devils and oral panics: The creation of mods and rockers.* Oxford, England: Blackwell.

Conley, D. (1999). *Being Black, living in the red: Race, wealth, and social policy in America.* Berkeley, CA: University of California Press.

Cross, C. T. (2004). *Political education: National policy comes of age.* New York, NY: Teachers College Press.

Danzberger, J. P. (1992). School boards: A troubled American institution. In J. P. Danzberger (Ed.), *Facing the challenge: The report of the Twentieth Century Fund Task Force on School Governance* (pp. 19–124). New York, NY: Twentieth Century Fund.

Danzberger, J. P. (1994). Governing the nation's schools: The case for restructuring local school boards. *Phi Delta Kappan, 75,* 367–373.

Danzberger, J. P., Carol, L. N., Cunningham, L. L., Kirst, M. W., McCloud, B. A., & Usdan, M. D. (1987). School boards: The forgotten players on the education team. *Phi Delta Kappan, 69,* 53–59.

Danzberger, J. P., Kirst, M. W., & Usdan, M. D. (1992). *Governing public schools: New times, new requirements.* Washington, DC: Institute for Educational Leadership.

Danzberger, J. P., Kirst, M. W., & Usdan, M. D. (1993). *A framework for redefining the role and responsibilities of local school boards.* Washington, DC: Institute for Educational Leadership.

Davidson, A. L. (1996). *Making and molding identity in schools: Student narratives on race, gender and academic engagement.* New York, NY: SUNY Press.

Davidson, A. L., & Phelan, P. (1993). Cultural diversity and its implications for schooling: A continuing American dialogue. In P. Phelan & A. L. Davidson (Eds.), *Renegotiating cultural diversity in American schools* (pp. 1–26). New York, NY: Teachers College Press.

Deal, T. E., & Peterson, K. D. (1990). *The principal's role in shaping school culture.* Washington, DC: U.S. Government Printing Office.

Delgado-Gaitan, C. (1987). Traditions and transitions in the learning process of Mexican children: An ethnographic view. In G. Spindler & L. Spindler (Eds.), *Interpretive ethnography of education: At home and abroad* (pp. 333–359). Hillsdale, NJ: Erlbaum.

Delpit, L. (1995) *Other people's children.* New York, NY: New Press.

deMarrais, K. B., & LeCompte, M. D. (1999). *The way schools work: A sociological analysis of education.* White Plains, NY: Longman.

Durkheim, E. (1956). *Education and society.* New York, NY: Free Press.

Education Commission of the States. (2003, December). *Improving academic achievement in urban districts: What state policymakers can do.* Denver, CO: Author.

Elias, M. J., Zins, J. E., Weissberg, R.P., Frey, K. S., Greenberg, M. T., Haynes, N. M. … Shriver, T. P. (1997). *Promoting social and emotional learning: Guidelines for educators.* Alexandria, VA: Association for Supervision and Curriculum Development.

Elmore, R. (2000). *Building a new structure for school leadership.* Washington, DC: Albert Shanker Institute.

Epstein, J. S. (1998). Introduction: Generation X, youth culture, and identity. In J. S. Epstein (Ed.), *Youth culture: Identity in a postmodern world* (pp. 1–23). Malden, MA: Blackwell.

Erickson, F. D. (1987) Transformation and school success: The politics and culture of educational achievement. *Anthropology & Education Quarterly, 18*(4), 335–355.

Erickson, F. D., & Mohatt, G. (1982) Cultural organization in two classrooms of Indian students. In G. D. Spindler (Ed.), *Doing the ethnography of schooling: Educational anthropology in action* (pp. 132–175). New York, NY: Holt, Rinehart & Winston.

Ernst-Slavit, G., & Wenger, K. J. (2006) Teaching in the margins: The multifaceted work and struggle of bilingual paraeducators. *Anthropology & Education Quarterly, 37*(1), 62–82.

Fine, M. (1991). *Framing dropouts: Notes on the politics of an urban public high school.* Albany, NY: SUNY Press.

Fine, M. (1994a). Chartering urban school reform. In M. Fine (Ed.), *Chartering urban school reform: Reflections on public high schools in the midst of change* (pp. 5–30). New York, NY: Teachers College Press.

Fine, M. (1994b). Framing a reform movement. In M. Fine (Ed.), *Chartering urban school reform: Reflections on public high schools in the midst of change* (pp. 1–3). New York, NY: Teachers College Press.

Fine, M., & Weis, L. (1998). *The unknown city: The lives of poor and working-class young adults.* Boston, MA: Beacon Press.

Fordham, S. (1988) Racelessness in Black students' school success: Pragmatic strategy or pyrrhic victory? *Harvard Educational Review, 58*(1), 54–84.

Fordham, S. (1996). *Blacked out: Dilemmas of race, identity, and success at Capital High.* Chicago, IL: University of Chicago Press.

Fordham, S. (2008). Beyond Capital High: On dual citizenship and the strange career of "acting white." *Anthropology & Education Quarterly, 39*(3), 227–246.

Fordham, S., & Ogbu, J. U. (1986). Black students' school success: Coping with the "burden of acting white." *Urban Review, 18,* 176–206.

Freire, P. (1993). *Pedagogy of the oppressed.* New York, NY: Continuum. (Original work published 1970)

Fullan, M. (2001). *Leading in a culture of change.* San Francisco, CA: Jossey-Bass.

Fullan, M. (2007). *The new meaning of educational change.* New York, NY: Teachers College Press.

Fullan, M., & Hargreaves, A. (1992). *What's worth fighting for: Working together for your school.* New York, NY: Teachers College Press.

Garot, R. (2010). *Who you claim: Performing gang identity in school and on the streets.* New York, NY: New York University Press.

Gay, G. (2000). *Culturally responsive teaching: Theory, research, and practice.* New York, NY: Teachers College Press.

Gibson, D. E., & Barasade, S. G. (2003). Managing organizational change: The case of long-term care. *Journal of Social Work in Long-term Care, 2,* 11–34.

Giroux, H. A. (1983). *Theory of resistance: A pedagogy for the opposition.* South Hadley, MA: Bergin & Garvey.

Giroux, H. A. (1998). Teenage sexuality, body politics, and the pedagogy of display. In J. S. Epstein (Ed.), *Youth culture: Identity in a postmodern world* (pp. 24–55). Malden, MA: Blackwell.

Gonsalves, L., & Leonard, J. (2007). *New hope for urban high schools: Cultural reform, moral leadership, and community partnership.* Westport, CT: Praeger.

Goodlad, J. (1975). *The dynamics of educational change.* New York, NY: McGraw-Hill.

Goodman, R. H., & Zimmerman, W. G. (2000). *Thinking differently: Recommendations for 21st century school board/superintendent leadership, governance, and teamwork for high student achievement.* Arlington, VA: Educational Research Service.

Gordon, E. T. (1997). Cultural politics of black masculinity. *Transforming Anthropology, 6*(1&2), 36–53.

Gordon, M. M. (1964) *Assimilation in American life.* New York, NY: Oxford University Press.

Grant, G. (1988). *The world we created at Hamilton High.* Cambridge, MA: Harvard University Press.

Greenleaf, R. (1991). *Servant leadership.* New York, NY: Paulist Press.

Grenfell, M., & James, D. (1998). *Bourdieu and education: Acts of practical theory.* Bristol, PA: Falmer.

Guajardo, M., & Guajardo, F. (2008) Transforming education: Chronicling a pedagogy for social change. *Anthropology & Education Quarterly, 39*(1), 3–22.

Hall, K. D. (2002) *Lives in translation: Sikh youth as British citizens.* Philadelphia, PA: University of Pennsylvania Press.

Heath, S. B. (1983). *Ways with words: Language, life and work in communities and classrooms.* New York, NY: Cambridge University Press.

Hemmings, A. (1996). Conflicting images? Being Black and a model high school student. *Anthropology & Education Quarterly, 27*(1), 20–50.

Hemmings, A. (1998). The self transformations of African-American achievers. *Youth & Society, 29*(2), 330–368.

Hemmings, A. (2000a). The "hidden" corridor curriculum. *The High School Journal, 83*(2), 1–10.

Hemmings, A. (2000b). Lona's links: Postoppositional identity work of urban youths. *Anthropology & Education Quarterly, 31*(2), 152–172.

Hemmings, A. (2002). Youth culture of hostility: Discourses of money, respect, and difference. *International Journal of Qualitative Studies in Education, 15*(3), 291–307.

Hemmings, A. (2003). Fighting for respect in urban high schools. *Teachers College Record, 105*(3), 416–437.

Hemmings, A. (2004). *Coming of age in U.S. high schools: Economic, kinship, religious, and political crosscurrents.* Mahwah, NJ: Erlbaum.

Hemmings, A. (2006a). Moral order in high school authority: Dis/enabling care and (un)scrupulous achievement. In J. Pace & A. Hemmings (Eds.), *Classroom authority: Theory, research, and practice* (pp. 135–150). Mahwah, NJ: Erlbaum.

Hemmings, A. (2006b). Shifting images of Blackness: Coming of age as Black students in urban and suburban high schools. In E. M. Horvat & C. O'Connor (Eds.), *Beyond acting white: Reframing the debate on Black student achievement* (pp. 91–110). Lanham, MD: Rowman & Littlefield.

Hemmings, A. (2007). Seeing the light: Cultural and social capital productions in an inner-city high school. *The High School Journal, 90*(3), 9–17.

Henderson, R. D. (2004) Teacher unions: Continuity and change. In R. D. Henderson, W. J. Urban, & P. Wolman (Eds.), *Teacher unions and educational policy: Retrenchment or reform?* (pp. 1–32). Amsterdam, the Netherlands: Elsevier.

Henderson, R. D., Urban, W. J., & Wolman, P. (2004). Introduction. In R. D. Henderson, W. J. Urban, & P. Wolman (Eds.), *Teacher unions and educational policy: Retrenchment or reform?* (pp. xi–xxix). Amsterdam, the Netherlands: Elsevier.

Hoffman, D. M. (1998). A therapeutic moment? Identity, self and culture in the anthropology of education. *Anthropology & Education Quarterly, 29*(3), 324–346.

Hoffman-Johnson, G. (2007). Seamless transition in the twenty-first century: Partnering to survive and thrive. *New Directions for Community Colleges, 139*, 17–27.

Horvat, E. M., & O'Connor, C. (2006) *Beyond acting white: Reframing the debate on Black student achievement*. Lanham, MD: Rowman & Littlefield.

Hoyle, J. R., Bjork, L. G., Collier, V., & Glass, T. (2005). *The superintendent as CEO: Standards-based performances*. Thousand Oaks, CA: Corwin Press

Ingersoll, R. M. (2001). Teacher turnover and teacher shortages: An organization analysis. *American Educational Research Journal, 38*(3), 499–534.

Jacob. E., & Jordan, C. (1993) Understanding educational anthropology: Concepts and methods. In E. Jacob & C. Jordan (Eds.), *Minority education: Anthropological perspectives* (pp. 15–24). Norwood, NJ: Ablex.

Johnson, S. M. (2004). Paralysis or possibility: What do teacher unions and collective bargaining bring? In R. D. Henderson, W. J. Urban, & P. Wolman (Eds.), *Teacher unions and educational policy: Retrenchment or reform?* (pp. 33–50). Amsterdam, the Netherlands: Elsevier.

Joyce, B. R., Hersh, R. H., & McKibbon, M. (1983). *The structure of school improvement*. New York, NY: Longman.

Kasinitz, P., Mollenkopf, J. H., Waters, M. C., & Holdaway, J. (2008). *Inheriting the city: The children of immigrants come of age*. New York, NY: Russell Sage Foundation.

Kay, J. (1993). *Foundations of corporate success*. Oxford, UK: Oxford University Press.

Kimball, R. (2000). *The long march: How the cultural revolution of the 1960s changed America*. San Francisco, CA: Encounter Books.

Kowalksi, T. J. (2005). *The school superintendent: Theory, practice, and cases*. Thousand Oaks, CA: Sage.

Kozol, J. (1967). *Death at an early age*. Boston, MA: Houghton-Mifflin.

Kübler-Ross, E. (1970). The care of the dying: Whose job is it? *Psychiatry in Medicine, 1*, 103–107.

Kuh, G. D., & Whitt, E. J. (1998). *The invisible tapestry: Culture in American colleges and universities* (ASHE-ERIC Higher Education Report, 1998, no.1). Washington, DC: Association for the Study of Higher Education.

Land, D. (2002) Local school boards under review: Their role and effectiveness in relation to students' academic achievement. *Review of Educational Research, 72*(2), 229–278.

Lareau, A. (2001). Linking Bourdieu's concept of capital to the broader field: The case of family–school relationships. In B. J. Biddle (Ed.), *Social class, poverty, and education: Policy and practice* (pp. 77–100). New York, NY: Routledge/Falmer.

Lesko, N. (1988). The curriculum of the body: Lessons from a Catholic high school. In L. Roman & L. K. Christian-Smith (Eds.), *Becoming feminine: The politics of popular culture* (pp. 123–142). New York, NY: Falmer Press.

Levinson, B. A., & Holland, D. C. (1996). The cultural production of the educated person: An introduction. In B. A. Levinson, D. E. Foley, & D. C. Holland (Eds.), *The cultural production of the educated person: Critical ethnographies of schooling and local practice* (pp. 1–54) Albany, NY: SUNY Press.

Li, G., & Wang, L. (2008). *Model minority myth revisited: An interdisciplinary approach to demystifying Asian American education experiences*. Charlotte, NC: Information Age.

Lieberman, A., & Miller, L. (2004). *Teacher leadership*. San Francisco, CA: Jossey-Bass.

Littlejohn, S. (2002). *Theories of Human Communication*. Albuquerque, NM: Wadsworth.

Logan, J. R., & Deane, G. (2003). *Black diversity in metropolitan America: Report for the Lewis Mumford Center for Comparative Urban and Regional Research*. Albany, NY: SUNY Press.

Long, N. E. (1958). The local community as an ecology of games. *American Journal of Sociology, 64*(3), 251–261.

Lortie, D. (1975). *School teacher: A sociological study*. Chicago, IL: University of Chicago Press.

Madison, D. S. (2005). *Critical ethnography: Method, ethics, and performance*. Thousand Oaks, CA: Sage.

Marcus, G., & Fischer, M. (1986). *Anthropology as cultural critique: An experimental moment in the human sciences.* Chicago, IL: University of Chicago Press.

Marwick, A. (1998). *The sixties: Cultural revolution in Britain, France, Italy, and the United States, c. 1958–1974.* Oxford, England: Oxford University Press.

Matute-Bianchi, M. E. (1991). Situational ethnicity and patterns of school performance among immigrant and nonimmigrant Mexican-descent students. In M. A. Gibson & J. U. Ogbu (Eds.), *Minority status and schooling: A comparative study of immigrant and involuntary minorities* (pp. 205–247). New York, NY: Garland.

McCarthy, M. M. (1985). Religion and public schools: Emerging legal standards and unresolved issues. *Harvard Educational Review, 55*(3), 278–317.

McDermott, R. P. (1974). Achieving school failure: An anthropological approach to illiteracy and social stratification. In G. D. Spindler (Ed.), *Education and cultural process: Toward an anthropology of education* (pp. 173–209). New York, NY: Holt, Rinehart & Winston.

McGuinn, P. J. (2006). *No Child Left Behind and the transformation of federal education policy, 1965–2005.* Lawrence: University Press of Kansas.

McNeil, L. M. (1983). Defensive teaching and classroom control. In M. W. Apple & L. Weis (Eds.), *Ideology & practice in schooling* (pp. 114–142). Philadelphia, PA: Temple University Press.

McNeil, L. (1986). *Contradictions of control: School structure and school knowledge.* New York: Routledge and Kegan Paul.

Metz, M. H. (1978). *Classrooms and corridors: The crisis of authority in desegregated secondary schools.* Berkeley, CA: University of California Press.

Metz, M. H. (1990). Real school: A universal drama amid disparate experience. In D. Mitchell & M. Goertz (Eds.), *Politics of education association yearbook* (pp. 75–91). London: Taylor & Francis.

Metz, M. H. (1993). Teachers' ultimate dependence on their students. In J. W. Little & M. W. McLaughlin (Eds.), *Teachers' work: Individuals, colleagues and contexts* (pp. 104–136). New York, NY: Teachers College Press.

Meyer, J., & Rowan, B. (1983) The structure of educational organizations. In J. V. Baldridge & T. Deal (Eds.), *The dynamics of organizational change in education* (pp. 60–88). Berkeley, CA: McCutchan.

Meyer, M., & Zucker, L. (1989). *Permanently Failing Organizations.* Newbury Park, NY: Sage.

Michie, G. (1999). *Holler if you hear me: The education of a teacher and his students.* New York, NY: Teachers College Press.

Mittelberg, D., & Waters, M. C. (1992). The process of ethnogenesis among Haitian and Israeli immigrants in the United States. *Ethnic and Racial Studies, 15,* 412–435.

Naff, A. (1985). *Becoming American: The early Arab immigrant experience.* Carbondale, IL: Southern Illinois University Press.

Naff, A. (1994). The early Arab immigrant experience. In E. McCarus (Ed.), *The development of Arab-American identity* (pp. 25–35). Ann Arbor, MI: University of Michigan Press.

Newman, W. A. (1973). *American pluralism: A study of minority groups in social theory.* New York, NY: Harper & Row.

Noddings, N. (1984). *Caring: A feminine approach to ethics and morality.* Berkeley, CA: University of California Press.

Noddings, N (1999). Two concepts of caring. *PES Yearbook.* Retrieved from http://www.edu.uiuc.edu/EPS/PES-Yearbook/1999/noddings_body.asp

Oakes, J. (1985). *Keeping track: How schools structure inequality.* New Haven, CT: Yale University Press.

Oakes, J., Quartz, K., Ryan, S., & Lipton, M. (1999). *Becoming good American schools.* San Francisco, CA: Jossey-Bass.

O'Connor, C. (1997). Dispositions toward (collective) struggle and educational resilience in the inner city: A case analysis of six African-American high school students. *American Educational Research Journal, 34,* 593–629.

Ogbu, J. U. (1978). *Minority education and caste: The American system in cross-cultural perspective.* New York, NY: Academic Press.

Ogbu, J. U. (1987). Variability in minority school performance: A problem in search of a solution. *Anthropology & Education Quarterly, 18,* 313–334.

Ogbu, J. U. (1991). Minority coping responses and school experience. *The Journal of Psychohistory, 18*(4), 433–456.

Ogbu, J. U. (1995a). Cultural problems in minority education: The interpretations and consequences. Part one: Theoretical background. *The Urban Review, 27,* 189–205.

Ogbu, J. U. (1995b). Problems in minority education: Their interpretations and consequences. Part two: Case studies. *The Urban Review, 27,* 271–297.

Ogbu, J. U. (2003). *Black American students in an affluent suburb: A study of academic disengagement.* Mahwah, NJ: Erlbaum.

Ogbu, J. U., & Simons, H. D. (1998). Voluntary and involuntary minorities: A cultural–ecological theory of school performance with some implications for education. *Anthropology & Education Quarterly, 29,* 155–188.

Omi, M., & Winant, H. (1994). *Racial formation in the United States.* New York, NY: Routledge.

Orfield, G. (1978). *Must we bus? Segregated schools and national policy.* Washington, DC: Brookings Institute.

Orfield, G. (2000). The 1964 Civil Rights Act and American education. In B. Grofman (Ed.), *Legacies of the 1964 Civil Rights Act* (pp. 89–128). Charlottesville, VA: University Press of Virginia.

Orfield, G., Eaton, S. E., & the Harvard Project on School Desegregation. (1996). *Dismantling desegregation: The quiet reversal of Brown v. Board of Education.* New York, NY: New Press.

O'Reilly, C., & Chatman, J. A. (1996). Culture as social control: Corporations, cults, and commitment. In B. M. Staw & L. L. Cummings (Eds.), *Research in organizational behavior* (pp. 157–200). Stamford, CT: JAI Press.

Pace, J. (1998). *Authority relationships in diverse high school classrooms* (Unpublished doctoral dissertation). Harvard University, Cambridge, MA.

Pace, J. (2003). Managing the dilemmas of professional and bureaucratic authority in a high school English class. *Sociology of Education, 76,* 37–52.

Pace, J. (2006). Saving (and losing) face, race, and authority: Strategies of action in a 9th grade English class. In J. L. Pace & A. Hemmings (Eds.), *Classroom authority: Theory, research, and practice* (pp. 87–112). Mahwah, NJ: Erlbaum.

Pace, J., & Hemmings, A. (Eds.). (2006a). *Classroom authority: Theory, research, and practice.* Mahwah, NJ: Erlbaum.

Pace, J., & Hemmings, A. (2006b). Preface. In J. Pace & A. Hemmings (Eds.), *Classroom authority: Theory, research, and practice* (pp. xi–xvi). Mahwah, NJ: Erlbaum.

Pace, J., & Hemmings, A. (2006c). Understanding classroom authority as a social construction. In J. Pace & A. Hemmings (Eds.), *Classroom authority: Theory, research, and practice* (pp. 1–31). Mahwah, NJ: Erlbaum.

Pace, J., & Hemmings, A. (2007). Understanding authority in classrooms: A review of theory, ideology, and research. *Review of Educational Research, 77*(1), 4–27.

Page, R. N. (1990). A "relevant" lesson: Defining the lower-track student. In R. Page & L. Valli (Eds.), *Curriculum differentiation: Interpretive studies in U.S. secondary schools* (pp. 17–43). Albany, NY: SUNY Press.

Page, R. N., & Valli, L. (1990) Curriculum differentiation: An introduction. In R. Page & L. Valli (Eds.), *Curriculum differentiation: Interpretive studies in U.S. secondary schools* (pp. 1–15). Albany, NY: SUNY Press.

Page, D., & Wong, T. P. (2000). A conceptual framework for measuring servant leadership. In S. Adjibolosoo (Ed.), *The human factor in shaping the course of history and development* (pp. 1–28). Lanham, MD: University Press of America.

Pai, Y. (1990). *Cultural foundations of education.* New York, NY: Macmillan.

Palmer, B., Walls, M., Burgess, Z., & Stough, C. (2001). Emotional intelligence and effective leadership. *Leadership and Development Journal, 22*(1), 5–10.

Parsons, T. (1947). Introduction. In *Max Weber: The theory of social and economic organization* (pp. 1–86). Glencoe, IL: Free Press.

Parsons, T. (1959). The school class as a social system: Some of its functions in American society. *Harvard Educational Review, 4,* 297–318.

Parsons, T. (1964). *Essays in sociological theory.* Chicago, IL: Free Press.

Payne, C. M. (2008). *So much reform, so little change: The persistence of failure in urban schools.* Cambridge, MA: Harvard Education Press.

Percell, C. H. (1977). *Education and inequality.* New York, NY: Free Press.

Pew Research Center. (2010). New Pew forum on religion and public life. Retrieved from http://religions.pewforum.org/affiliations

Phelan, P., & Davidson, A. L. (1993). *Renegotiating cultural diversity in American schools.* New York, NY: Teachers College Press.

Phelan, P., Davidson, A. L., & Yu, H. C. (1993) Students' multiple worlds: Navigating the borders of family, peer, and school cultures. In P. Phelan & A. L. Davidson (Eds.), *Renegotiating cultural diversity in American schools* (pp. 52–88). New York, NY: Teachers College Press.

Phelan, P., Davidson, A. L., & Yu, H. C. (1998). *Adolescents' worlds: Negotiating family, peers, and school.* New York, NY: Teachers College Press.

Philips, S. U. (1983). *The invisible culture: Communication in classroom and community on the Warm Springs Indian Reservation.* White Plains, NY: Longman.

Portes, A., & Zhou, M. (1993). The new second generation: Segmented assimilation and its variants. *Annals of the American Political and Social Sciences, 530,* 74–96.

Queen, J. A. (2008). *The block scheduling handbook.* Thousand Oaks, CA: Corwin Press.

Raisiguier, C. (1994). *Becoming women, becoming workers: Identity formation in a French vocation school.* Albany, NY: SUNY Press.

Ravitch, D. (2010). *The death and life of the great American school system: How testing and choice are undermining education.* New York, NY: Basic Books.

Reed-Danahay, D. (2005). *Locating Bourdieu.* Bloomington, IN: Indiana University Press.

Resnick, M. A. (1999) *Effective school governance: A look at today's practice and tomorrow's promise.* Denver, CO: Education Commission of the States.

Rhodes, V., Stevens, D., & Hemmings, A. (2011). Creating positive culture in a new urban high school. *The High School Journal, 94*(3), 82–94.

Robbins, D. (2000). *Bourdieu and culture.* Thousand Oaks, CA: Sage.

Rodriguez, R. (1982). *Hunger of memory: The education of Richard Rodriquez.* New York, NY: Bantam Books.

Rogers, D. (1969). *110 Livingston Street: Politics and bureaucracy in the New York City school system.* New York, NY: Vintage.

Rosario, J. R. (2000). Communitarianism and the moral order of schools. In B. M. Franklin (Ed.), *Curriculum and consequence: Herbert M. Kliebard and the promise of schooling* (pp. 30–51). New York, NY: Teachers College Press.

Rosenfeld, G. (1971). *"Shut those thick lips!" A study of slum school failure.* New York, NY: Holt, Rinehart, & Winston.

Rothman, R. (1992). Boards of contention: Historians cite "steady erosion" in local control. *Education Week, 11*(32), 4–5.

Rueda, R., & DeNeve, C. (1999) How paraeducators build cultural bridges in diverse classrooms. *Reaching Today's Youth: Community Circle of Caring Journal, 3*(2), 53–55.

Rutter, M., Maughan, B., Mortimore, P., & Ouston, J. (1979). *Fifteen thousand hours: Secondary schools and their effects on children.* Cambridge, MA: Harvard University Press.

Ryan, W. (1972) *Blaming the victim.* New York, NY: Vintage Books.

Sadovnik, A. R., Cookson, Jr., P. W., & Semel, S. F. (2001). *Exploring education: An introduction to the foundations of education.* Boston, MA: Allyn & Bacon.

Sarason, S. B. (1996). *Revisiting "the culture of the school and the problem of change."* New York, NY: Teachers College Press.

Sarroub, L. K. (2005). *All American Yemeni girls: Being a Muslim in a public school.* Philadelphia, PA: University of Pennsylvania Press.

Schein, E. H. (1991). *Organizational culture and leadership.* San Francisco, CA: Jossey-Bass.

Seller, M., & Weis, L. (1998). Immigrants and education: An introduction. [Special issue] *Educational Policy, 12,* 611–614.

Selznick, P. (1992). *The moral commonwealth: Social theory and the promise of community.* Berkeley: University of California Press.

Senge, P. (1990). The leader's new work: Building learning organizations. *Sloan Management Review, 32,* 7–23.

Shulman, L. S. (2000). Teacher development: Roles of domain expertise and pedagogical knowledge. *Journal of Applied Developmental Psychology, 21*(1), 129–135.

Shust, D., & Lewis, C. (2004) The National Education Association's new bipartisanship. In R. D. Henderson, W. J. Urban, & P. Wolman (Eds.), *Teacher unions and educational policy: Retrenchment or reform?* (pp. 81–102) Amsterdam, the Netherlands: Elsevier.

Sirotnik, K. A., & Goodlad, J. I. (1988). *School–university partnerships in action: Concepts, cases, and Concerns.* New York, NY: Teachers College Press.

Sizer, T. R., & Sizer, N. F. (1999). *The students are watching: Schools and the moral contract.* Boston, MA: Beacon Press.

Skerrett, A., & Hargreaves, A. (2008). Student diversity and secondary school change in a context of increasingly standardized reform. *American Educational Research Journal, 45*(4), 913–945.

Slater, J. J. (1996) *Anatomy of a collaboration: Study of a college of education/public school partnership.* New York, NY: Garland.

Spindler, G. (1978). *The making of psychological anthropology.* Berkeley: University of California Press.

Spindler, G. (1999). Three categories of cultural knowledge useful for doing cultural therapy. *Anthropology & Education Quarterly, 30*(4), 466–472.

Spindler, G. (2002). The collusion of illusions and how to get people to tell you what they don't know. In Y. Zou & E. T.Trueba (Eds.), *Ethnography and schools: Qualitative approaches to the study of education* (pp. 13–26). Lanham, MD: Rowman & Littlefield.

Spindler, G., & Spindler, L. (1992). The enduring, situated, and endangered self in fieldwork: A personal account. In B. Boyer (Ed.), *The psychoanalytical study of society* (pp. 23–28). Hillsdale, NJ: Analytic Press.

Spindler, G., & Spindler, L. (1993). The processes of culture and person: Cultural therapy and culturally diverse schools. In P. Phelan & A. L. Davidson (Eds.), *Renegotiating cultural diversity in American schools* (pp. 27–51). New York, NY: Teachers College Press.

Spring, J. (2010). *Political agendas for education: From change we can believe in to putting America first.* New York, NY: Routledge.

Staiger, A. D. (2006). *Learning difference: Race and schooling in the multiracial metropolis.* Stanford, CA: Stanford University Press.

Shweder, R. A. (1991). *Thinking through cultures: Expeditions in cultural psychology.* Cambridge, MA: Harvard University Press.

Swidler, A. (1979). *Organization without authority: Dilemmas of social control in free schools.* Cambridge, MA: Harvard University Press.

Swidler, A. (1986). Culture in action: Symbols and strategies. *American Sociological Review, 51,* 273–286.

Trueba, E. T. (1988). Culturally based explanations of minority students' academic achievement. *Anthropology & Education Quarterly, 19,* 270–281.

Trueba, E. T. (1993). *Healing multicultural America: Mexican immigrants rise to power in rural California.* Washington, DC: Falmer.

Trueba, E. T., Spindler, G., & Spindler, L. (1988). *What do anthropologists have to say about dropouts?* New York, NY: Falmer.

Trujillo, A. (1996). In search of Aztlan: *Movimento* ideology and the creation of a Chicano world-view through schooling. In B. A. Levinson, D. E. Foley, & D. C. Holland (Eds.), *The cultural production of the educated person: Critical ethnographies of schooling and local practice* (pp. 119–152). Albany, NY: SUNY Press.

Tyack, D. B. (1974). *The one best system: A history of American urban education.* Cambridge, MA: Harvard University Press.

Valenzuela, A. (1999). *Subtractive schooling: U.S.-Mexican youth and the politics of caring.* New York, NY: SUNY Press.

Vinovskis, M. A. (2009). *From a Nation at Risk to No Child Left Behind: National education goals and the creation of federal education policy.* New York, NY: Teachers College Press.

Waller, W. (1961). *The sociology of teaching.* New York, NY: Wiley. (Original work published 1932)

Waters, M. C. (1999). *Black identities: West Indian immigrant dreams and American realities.* New York, NY: Russell Sage Foundation.

Watras, J. (2008). *A history of American education.* Boston, MA: Pearson.

Weber, M. (1947). *The theory of social and economic organization.* New York, NY: Oxford University Press. (Original work published 1925)

Weick, K. (1983). Educational organizations as loosely coupled systems. In J. V. Baldridge & T. Deal (Eds.), *The dynamics of organizational change in education* (pp. 15–37). Berkeley, CA: McCutchan.

Weiner, L. (1993). *Preparing teachers for urban schools: Lessons from thirty years of reform.* New York, NY: Teachers College Press.

Weiner, L. (1999). *Urban teaching: The essentials.* New York, NY: Teachers College Press.

Weiner, L. (2000). Research in the 90s: Implications for urban teacher preparation. *Review of Educational Research, 70*(30), 369–406.

Weiner, L (2006). *Urban teaching: The essentials.* New York, NY: Teachers College Press.

Weis, L. & Fine, M. (2000). *Construction sites: Excavating race, class and gender among urban youths.* New York, NY: Teachers College Press.

Willis, P. (1977). *Learning to labour: How working-class kids get working-class jobs..* Farnborough, UK: Saxon House.

Wilson, J. W. (1996). *When work disappears: The world of the new urban poor.* New York, NY: Knopf.

Wong, K., & Nicotera, A. C. (2004). *Brown v. Board of Education* and the Coleman Report: Social science research and the debate on educational equality. *Peabody Journal of Education, 79,* 122–135.

Yon, D. A. (2000). *Elusive culture: Schooling, race, and identity in global times.* New York, NY: SUNY Press.

Zane, N. (1994). When "discipline problems" recede: Democracy and intimacy in urban charters. In M. Fine (Ed.), *Chartering urban school reform: Reflections on public high schools in the midst of change* (pp. 122–135). New York, NY: Teachers College Press.

Zimpher, N. L., & Howey, K. R. (2004). System-to-system reform of teacher education and school renewal. In N. L. Zimpher & K. R. Howey (Eds.), *University leadership in urban school renewal* (pp. 105–129). Westport, CT: Praeger.

Zins, J. E., & Elias, M. J. (2007). *Bullying, victimization and peer harassment: A handbook of prevention and intervention.* Binghamton, NY: Haworth.

INDEX